Ethics and Burial Archaeology

D1461411

BRISTOL CLASSICAL PRESS DEBATES IN ARCHAEOLOGY

Series editor: Richard Hodges

Against Cultural Property John Carman
Archaeology: The Conceptual Challenge Timothy Insoll
Archaeology and Text John Moreland
Archaeology and the Pan-European Romanesque
Tadhg O'Keeffe
Beyond Celts, Germans and Scythians Peter S. Wells
Combat Archaeology John Schofield
Debating the Archaeological Heritage Robin Skeates
Early Islamic Syria Alan Walmsley
Gerasa and the Decapolis David Kennedy
Image and Response in Early Europe Peter S. Wells
Indo-Roman Trade Roberta Tomber
Loot, Legitimacy and Ownership Colin Renfrew
Lost Civilization James L. Boone
The Origins of the English Catherine Hills
Rethinking Wetland Archaeology Robert Van de Noort &
Aidan O'Sullivan
The Roman Countryside Stephen Dyson
Shipwreck Archaeology of the Holy Land Sean Kingsley
Social Evolution Mark Pluciennik
State Formation in Early China Li Liu & Xingcan Chen
Towns and Trade in the Age of Charlemagne
Richard Hodges
Villa to Village Riccardo Francovich & Richard Hodges

Ethics and Burial Archaeology

Duncan Sayer

Bristol Classical Press

2014002969

Published by Bristol Classical Press 2012

Bristol Classical Press, an imprint of Bloomsbury Publishing Plc

Bloomsbury Publishing Plc
50 Bedford Square
London WC1B 3DP
www.bloomsburyacademic.com

Copyright © Duncan Sayer 2010

First published by Gerald Duckworth & Co. Ltd.2010

The author has asserted his rights under the Copyright, Designs and
Patents Act 1988 to be identified as the author of this work.

ISBN: 978 0 715 63893 4

A CIP catalogue record for this book is available from the British Library

Typeset by Ray Davies
Printed and bound in Great Britain by CPI Group (UK) Ltd, Croydon, CR0 4YY

This book is produced using paper that is made from wood grown in managed,
sustainable forests. It is natural, renewable and recyclable. The logging and
manufacturing processes conform to the environmental regulations of the
country of origin.

'If these bones lie at peace civilisation may surely rest.'
Bernard Levin, *The Times*, 11 January 1984

Contents

Preface   9
Acknowledgements   11
List of Figures   12

Introduction   13
1. Archaeology and exhumation   21
2. Archaeology, heritage and British burial law   45
3. Human decency, politics and digging the dead   70
4. Display, repatriation and respect for the dead   95
Conclusion: the problem of modernity and the
     ancient dead   127

Bibliography   139
Index   153

For my parents Sue and Phil Sayer

Preface

This book is perhaps best seen as the natural amalgamation of several different areas of my professional life. When I first graduated as an archaeologist I worked extensively in Sheffield and was involved directly or indirectly in the exhumation of several post-medieval cemeteries, including Carver Street Methodist Chapel, Barnsley New Street, St Paul's and Sheffield Cathedral. I then left to pursue an MA in Death and Society, a fabulous opportunity to combine archaeology and sociology and to think carefully about what the dead mean to people outside an archaeological framework. In the year between my MA and my PhD I directed aspects of the King's Cross St Pancras project, and again had the opportunity to meet the dead first-hand (the St Pancras project saw the removal of graves from Old St Pancras churchyard to allow the extension of a railway platform for Eurostar trains). I must admit the combination of St Pancras and my experience at Sheffield required me to consider very carefully what we, as archaeologists, were doing and why. I still look back at that Master's programme fondly, and now several years later I contribute to a similar programme at the University of Bath. The aim is the same, to combine different disciplines and different ways of thinking about death, dying and the dead into a single central postgraduate course at the Centre for Death and Society.

However, this book is also the result of a number of different seminar classes that I ran at the University of Bath and the University of Reading from 2005 to the time of writing. These focused on the question of ethics and burial archaeology and used some of the case studies I present here to explore the diversity, context and history of the question. Addressing two groups, archaeologists and non-archaeologists, provided me with an insight into the subject which I think it would have been impossible to achieve if I had focused on a single subject and preached only to the 'choir'. Contained within this volume are a series of thoughts, histories, contexts and ideas which I hope readers will find as useful and interesting as I did during their initial discussion.

I have always intended this book to be an accessible source of case studies which focus on British exhumation projects, but, just as projects in Australia, South Africa and America are of interest to students and scholars in the UK, archaeologists from all over the world will find its contents useful and informative; maybe even helpful in what can be challenging and sensitive circumstances. The legal material discussed is relevant to a UK context; however, the interaction between lawmakers and archaeologists and the history of this relationship have a much broader application to a global community of heritage professionals and burial archaeologists. Similar circumstances seem to repeat themselves within the global environment.

Acknowledgements

I would like to thank the Centre for Death and Society at the University of Bath for helping to fund this project and Deborah Blake, my editor at Duckworth, for her patience. I am grateful to Hugh Waterhouse for information on Sheffield's cemeteries; he is currently the chairman of the Friends of Walkley Cemetery. Cate Freiman and Sue Sayer usefully kept or sent various newspaper articles to me. I also appreciated discussions with Dave Evans concerning Joan Wytte, Tiffany Jenkins on museums, Mark Horton in relation to Rapparee Cove, Simon Mays about the law and archaeology and Phil Emery for discussing Arthur Dillon with me. Mary Beaudry and Bruce Watson both helpfully provided pre-publication material. Thanks must also go to Chris Gosden for commenting on the book proposal and Tony Walter, Giovanna Vitelli, Emma Gowans and Emma Restall Orr for reading drafts of this book and providing me with feedback or useful comments and corrections, which have improved the end result considerably. I would like to thank Michael Sadan of NI Syndication, Phyllis Stoddart of Manchester Museum, Anna Smith of Wellcome Images and Silke Wiegnad of the Körperwelten for permissions to use the images in this book. I would particularly like to thank Meredith Carroll for reading and commenting on the structure and presentation of the book, and Victoria Leitch who edited and commented on various drafts of the text in her usual professional and insightful way. Despite this invaluable group of people, the ideas, opinions and mistakes within this volume remain entirely my own.

List of Figures

1. The growth of industrial Sheffield as shown by its
   size in 1750, 1800 and 1850.   24
2. A plan of modern Sheffield showing the location of
   fifteen historic cemetery sites.   28
3. Sheffield Cathedral in 1793.   33
4. 'The Dig Issue', a topical cartoon highlighting the
   plight of the tombless.   55
5. The number of times archaeology has been
   . mentioned in parliament over the last 100 years.   67
6. Sheffield Cathedral in 1993 during the Super Tram
   construction works.   85
7. A plastinated man playing chess.   99
8. Visitors experiencing the 'Skeletons' exhibition.   101
9. Manchester Museum's Lindow Man exhibition.   103

Introduction

This book is titled *Ethics and Burial Archaeology*, but it is about the relationships between the living and the dead. The dead and the living are physically different and so the relationship between the two is not like other human relationships. For a start the living cannot be remains. However, the dead are not, at least most of the time, objects or material culture. They are, in the words of one historian, 'past generations' (De Baets 2004). They are past people, individuals who experienced the world in a way we can attempt to perceive. Past people were human and so past and present populations are connected through a sense of a shared human experience, a sense of empathy that we do not have for inanimate objects and material culture. In this way the ancient dead represent a special type of archaeology, and ordinary heritage principles and laws do not apply in the same way as for less emotive objects. It is only occasionally asked if it is morally correct to display a hand axe or an ancient gold brooch from a society with no living descendants, but today museums in the UK are routinely asking if it is ethical to display human remains. One of the aims of this book is to differentiate between the post-Colonial, New World Aboriginal context, and a European ethics debate. This is important as the New World position is not the best place to start a discussion of ethics and human remains in Europe, as both mainstream and marginalised communities can both claim to be indigenous. Moreover, in this context the use of 'indigenous' as an identity to strengthen a claim to ancient remains is in itself an act of ethnic exclusion, removing other important community and religious groups from the discussion.

Introduction

The dead are more than archaeology, they are the past, they lived in it and they were, or perhaps represent, all the people who have been. In this way our ancestors transcend academic or field archaeologists' interests. This book is also about the relationship between the living and the living, where the dead are inert catalysts used in that relationship, good or bad. In this way the role of burial archaeology and its impact on society is an issue that goes beyond archaeologically specific ethics (e.g. Scarre & Scarre 2006); broader social situations need to be taken into account. The use of the dead as an agent in society is a matter of historical record, not a new phenomenon. In pre- and proto-history people positioned graves and houses close to their ancient dead to create continuities. In the middle ages the dead were used as a means to justify the power of religions, and as a way to meet saints, or their relics, and witness miracles. This spiritual relationship still exists today and when the relics of St Thérèse of Lisieux came to Britain in 2009, 150,000 people visited them during a month-long tour (Moss 2009).

Equally the dead have been used as powerful tools by disenfranchised groups to change and liberate society. The late nineteenth-century Arkenham burial case is a good example. A deceased Baptist boy was refused the right to a funeral ceremony in a churchyard by a local high church rector because he had not been baptised, and so he was 'buried like a dog'. The subsequent scandal and public outcry was reported in the local and national press and as a result of the popular protest the law was changed in 1880 to allow Nonconformists (for example Baptists and Methodists) the right to a funeral performed by their own lay ministers in the local parish churchyard. The power of the Anglican Church to control the relationship of the living with their dead had been reduced (Sayer forthcoming; Fletcher 1974). In this way even today's medical scandals like that at Alder Hey, where pathologists retained children's remains without their parents' permission (see Chapter 2), have their historical context and represent a continuum for the political use of the dead by marginalised, and less marginal, social groups.

14

Introduction

The use of the dead in mainstream politics is well known; for example, Lenin, Stalin and Evita (Chamberlin & Parker Pearson 2001: 36-44; Verdery 1999: 23-53) were mummified or displayed to encourage the public impression of political stability in uncertain times. Even in recent western politics the dead play a role. French President Nicolas Sarkozy's ambition to rebury the remains of post-war intellectual Albert Camus under the Panthéon (alongside 'France's greatest heroes') was described by Camus' son as a cynical ploy to requisition his left-wing legacy (K. Hutton 2009). However, there is one case which highlights the problems discussed in this book better than most: the exhumation of John Henry Newman.

In 2008 Libby Purves, journalist, broadcaster, and also lapsed Catholic and religious critic, expressed her distaste at the attempts of the Birmingham Roman Catholic Church to exhume the body of John Henry Newman (Purves 2008). Newman was an important figure in the nineteenth-century Oxford Movement which saw the Anglican Church of England as a Catholic rather than Protestant Church and wanted to steer it back to its roots. He eventually converted to Catholicism and became a cardinal. In 1991 he was recognised as Venerable, and in 2008 Birmingham's Roman Catholic Church announced its intention to exhume his body to remove it to a marble tomb in the Oratory, so that his remains could be honoured while his case for canonisation was considered. This would separate his body from that of his lifelong companion, which many suggested was an expression of homophobia. It was also illegal, as among the Victorian burial laws which govern this area of modern life, is an injunction against urban intramural burial. An exception was made and, against Newman's own wishes 'to be buried in Father Ambrose St John's grave' (Purves 2008), they began exhumation. When grave diggers reached the site of Newman's body, however, due to localised ground conditions, nothing remained at all.

This story is not one of archaeologists conflicting with indigenous people, or other interest groups; however, it does encapsulate all the elements that many archaeologists experience. Libby Purves was and is quite happy to admit that she used this exhumation as a means to question the role of 'ghoulish' medieval traditions in modern religious practice, particularly Catholicism, a well-worn target for her journalism. The bones did not matter to her; similarly members of the gay rights movement used the exhumation as a way to highlight their dissatisfaction with traditional right-wing religions that do not recognise homosexuality as a legitimate lifestyle. Also the law was difficult to interpret and negotiate but not insurmountable, a familiar problem for many archaeologists in Britain, especially given the recent reinterpretation of the law (see Chapter 2). But even the Church was using the remains of one of its most influential past English churchmen as a means to attract pilgrims for veneration and raise its profile within Britain and across the Catholic world. It was securing its position as an important Church with a special connection to the saints by using and displaying the body of a man. So although in this case the bones did matter, the wishes of Newman himself did not. In all of these situations the living were more important than the dead, and to each of the agitators it was quite legitimate to use the dead for their own ambition, whether couched in terms of respect or not.

John Newman escaped his metamorphosis into a sacred object, and his body could not be exhumed, but within many cities, hundreds of skeletons are exhumed every year. Even in Birmingham others have not escaped exhumation and the recent Bull Ring project saw the removal of hundreds of bodies, not too far from the Church, to allow the redevelopment of the city centre and facilitate economic stability, or growth. The living were more important than the dead, they control the planning regulations and need jobs, clothes, food and social lives, whereas the dead do not. So maybe one of the questions in this book should not be *whether* archaeologists should exhume the dead, because this is inevitable: the nature of the relationship of the living with their past and the need for space in urban environments means that cemetery disturbance is unavoidable. Instead perhaps archaeologists should consider *how* to exhume the dead, since it is as a result of encounters with them that questions about respect and the interests of the living become known.

Within the British legal system is enshrined a need to respect the dead, as it is in other countries. But in few places is it defined. Archaeological codes of conduct, standards, guidelines and accords all require respect. Special interest groups, diaspora communities, indigenous people, Pagans, Catholics, Anglicans, Jews, Muslims and the general public all request and require the respectful treatment of the dead. Indeed many people discuss human dignity in different ways. For some it is to study and tell stories and so to remember past people and their societies; for others it is to avoid disturbing them at all so their bodies may remain intact and the afterlife unaffected; still others would ask for simple prayers or new rituals and ceremonies to be performed when the dead are exhumed. However, much of the disjunction that all of these groups feel is when there is a conflict, or exclusion. Still others use the terminology of respect for political ambitions to raise awareness of their community's voice or internal viewpoints. Geoffrey Scarre (2007: 129-30) has argued that it is impossible to accord needs to the dead and so it is impossible to respect those needs – the living cannot cause them pain, mental anguish, disappointment or embarrassment as we can people who are alive, although we can affect the esteem in which they are held or how they are remembered within living society.

So what does respect for the dead mean if it is not subjected to the needs of the living? In all the case studies I will illustrate in this book the connection is exclusion, which can engender suspicion, accusations of secretiveness and the idea that archaeologists are somehow meddling, fiddling or generally up to no good with the dead. In this context respect is about the needs and wishes of the living, and so means inclusion, openness and accountability, concepts not always easily associated with the hoardings that surround many exhumation projects.

The more recently deceased have been displayed in global exhibitions such as Gunther von Hagens' Body Worlds, but for the ancient dead, there are no permission slips and no donation forms. Perhaps as a result, museums are looking for authority, asking the museum-going public if they should display human remains. But while the role of the traditional museum is unclear and under question, human remains are being displayed outside the usual galleries in different institutions with different agendas, and to high acclaim. So perhaps, just as with exhumation, asking *whether* museum archaeologists should display human remains is the wrong question, and instead they should ask *how* to display them. Tony Walter (2004a) argued that display is a new form of disposal ranked alongside cremation and inhumation, and those museums and public displays are part of a culture's relationship with the dead, and importantly with death. With this significant social role there is no need to receive permission from the individual dead, as society's need provides authority; perhaps the dead are being honoured, and their lives remembered, as if they had been recently living.

The questions raised in this short introduction are dealt with in more detail throughout the book, and I will leave the question of what archaeologists can learn from the dead themselves to publications focused on physical anthropology or burial archaeology, for example Roberts (2009), Sayer & Williams (2009) and Parker Pearson (1999). This discussion is organised into five overlapping chapters which move through the processes of archaeology in a loosely chronological way. These chapters deal with why archaeologists excavate the dead and how they do it legally; the relationship between excavators and lawmakers, archaeologists, protesters and other interest groups; and the interaction between the public, museums and indigenous communities. It also focuses on the legality, exhumation, public display and repatriation of the dead under the umbrella of ethics in burial archaeology. By bringing all of these issues into one book I hope that this important debate which, at least in Britain, is primarily discussed in notes in journals, newsletters, through the media, and only occasionally in academic articles, will become more accessible, under-

Introduction

standable and productive for archaeologists and others alike. I
hope that my words will stimulate thought, discussion and
openness in areas where people have been suspicious and uncertain, and most of all I hope you do not agree with everything
I have written.

1

Archaeology and exhumation

Introduction

In 2004 De Baets outlined his 'declaration of the responsibilities of present generations toward past generations'. He approached the question of ethics and the dead from a distinctly historical perspective and his declaration aimed to place research into past populations within a human rights framework. De Baets outlines a number of responsibilities that living humans have towards 'previous humans' and indicates that while dead people have rights they are not the same rights as those of the living. However, the rest of this model is most useful when applied to the recently dead but tends towards a research-based situation, such as for historians who do not directly handle human remains and can select their own research agendas. However, not all the historical sciences, for example archaeology, are entirely research-driven and the vast majority of human remains excavated in the UK are a result of rescue excavations ahead of development programmes, and not part of an academic research agenda (Roberts 2009).

Despite the problems presented by De Baets' scheme, an ethical framework can still be constructed for rescue and commercial excavations, but it is important to understand how and why these investigations take place so that this perspective can be explored. In many modern contexts the dead are not as important as the living; they do not have the same human rights because they cannot speak for themselves. This is why their cemeteries can be, and are, developed; however, it is how they are developed that should be the focus for archaeologists and planners if they wish them to be approached within an ethically-driven agenda. For example, is it right to disregard the wishes of over a hundred dead Methodists who never drank alcohol by digging the foundations of a beer cellar where they were buried? Is it right to do that when a simple, but slightly more expensive, alternative is available and could result in the storage of that same alcohol away from the cemetery? By contrast, is it right to remove 1,000 human remains so that a new station platform can be built that will bring over £2 billion in regeneration money to an economically deprived city zone, and provide new jobs and new opportunities for disenfranchised and under-resourced people?

Society cannot simply ask 'who are more important, the living or the dead?' In modern secular societies the answer will almost always be the living: we control the budgets and the laws, we drive the diggers and plan the new towns. But it is also the living who create a special connection with the dead and who place special requirements on their treatment, defining how they should be buried, where they should be buried, and in European countries how long they should be buried for. However, the current British legal system which applies to the dead does not reflect this as it was not designed to consider historic cemeteries; these sites were contemporary when the laws were passed. The laws were designed in the nineteenth century to protect the living from exposure to the more unpleasant aspects of contemporary cemetery clearance. It is for these reasons that archaeologists need to rethink radically the way they go about cemetery archaeology.

This chapter outlines the history of cemetery exhumation projects, describes the pressure on building space, explains why it is important and why cemeteries are developed. I also discuss how these aspects must change and the need to develop an integrated system that allows voluntary public involvement in skeletal exhumation. Indeed, it is the public who go to see the results of these excavations in museums, so why should they be excluded from involvement in their excavation in order to protect their sensibilities?

Urban development and building space

To understand why archaeologists often encounter human remains it is important to illustrate briefly the growth of the UK's urban environment. To do this, Sheffield, South Yorkshire, will be used as an example (it will also be used later in this chapter to illustrate the scale of cemetery clearance in the UK's urban environment). This city makes a good case study as its development, and the development of its burial grounds, has been reasonably well documented over the last few years including periods of economic growth, decline and recovery.

Today the City of Sheffield has a population of c. 440,000, making it the fifth largest city in England (Office for National Statistics 2004). However, it has not always been that size: Fig. 1 shows Sheffield's development in 50-year increments, illustrating its growth between c. 1735 and c. 1850. The population of Sheffield trebled from 10,121 in 1736 to 31,314 in 1801 and more than doubled again to 83,446 in 1851 (Hey 1998: 91, 147). This industrial-period population then increased to 90,398 by 1901, by which time the city had spread beyond its original boundaries to include Ecclesall, Nether Hallam and Upper Hallam. This growth took place alongside the construction of large steelworks which augmented the centralised industries already present. Throughout the twentieth century the population remained constant in the city centre but spread outward. By 1945 it had covered an area of just over 10 square miles (Heys 1945) and today the population is c. 439,866 – or 640,720 if you include the entire urban area that annexes neighbouring towns such as Rotherham (Office for National Statistics 2004, also see SYHEC 2009).

By the mid-1960s 2,500 dwellings a year were being constructed in Sheffield, but this was not enough, and by 1972 a further 40,000 people needed to be housed outside the city (Hey 1998: 233). Between 1951 and 1991 an estimated 100,900 new homes were built and 55,000 old houses demolished (Hey 1998: 224). However, the collapse of the coal, steel and cutlery indus-

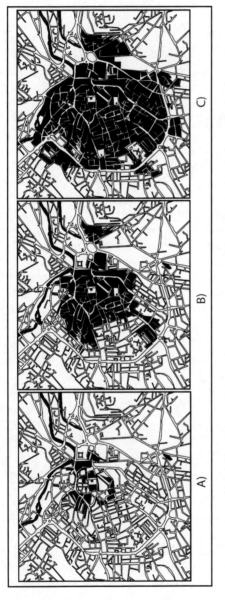

Fig. 1. (A) Sheffield before 1750, based on Gosling's map of 1736 superimposed on a modern map of Sheffield. The central area is c. 1 mile². (B) Sheffield before 1800, based on Fairbank's map of 1771 superimposed on a modern map of Sheffield. (C) Sheffield in 1850, based on the 1851 OS Map and superimposed on a modern map of Sheffield. In 1900 Sheffield extended beyond the boundaries of the base map used here.

tries in the 1970s and 1980s left the city in need of regeneration, as whole central areas were no longer in constant use. The city put together an economic regeneration plan, and in 1990 the American-style shopping centre Meadow Hall was opened. With this regeneration came science parks, leisure facilities and infrastructure projects such as the Super Tram and Transport Interchange. Between 1990 and 1996 over £300 million was invested in the city centre, followed by another £200 million by the millennium. As part of this continuous regeneration programme the Peace Gardens were reopened and the Winter Garden and Millennium Galleries added to them to make the city centre a pleasant space (Creative Sheffield 2007).

I am not trying to produce an exhaustive list of development work, but simply to demonstrate that these development projects are linked to economic survival. They highlight the relationship between urban success and development, which has existed since the late eighteenth century. Many of these early developments are now themselves regarded as part of the historic character of British cities and some buildings are of national importance. However, development work like this is common in other towns and cities, for example Manchester, Liverpool, Birmingham, Reading, Oxford and London, which places pressure on heritage preservation. Indeed, projects such as road widening, roundabouts and transport systems inevitably result in cemetery clearance where a modern emphasis on developing brown field sites (those that have previously been built on) and not new green fields (sites that have had no previous modern buildings) makes urban cemetery clearance inevitable (see Sayer & Symonds 2004).

Cemeteries and modern development

There is considerable diversity in cemetery sites found by archaeologists in Britain's urban environment: prehistoric funerary landscapes, Roman cemeteries, early Anglo-Saxon furnished cemeteries as well as medieval monastic, church and hospital cemeteries. But it is mainly the post-medieval sites that are visible today, which are the very sites now threatened by the pressures of modern development and urban infrastructure projects.

In the seventeenth century, after the English Reformation, burial in many monastic cemeteries was abolished, and new cemeteries, Protestant churches and cathedrals took on the responsibility for the majority of burials in the UK (Gilchrist 2003: 404). Shortly after the Glorious Revolution of 1688 (Houlbrooke 1999: 174) the right to free worship was established and with this new found freedom came the first private cemeteries; Quaker and other Presbyterian or Nonconformist groups established chapels and burial grounds. However, the greater part of the Nonconformist and Anglican population continued to be buried in parish churchyards, up until the nineteenth century. This placed a huge stress on the often small medieval churchyards as towns grew, and during the eighteenth and nineteenth centuries they were extended or relieved by satellite burial grounds on the edge of towns.

The diversification and increased popularity of the Nonconformist movement into the nineteenth century saw the establishment of new chapels, sometimes with burial grounds, and the construction of the Million Act Churches (The 1818 Million Act granted a million pounds for church construction around the country) at the beginning of the nineteenth century also helped to provide new burial space in Britain's growing industrial towns. However, overcrowding in parish churchyards was identified as one of the major risks to public wellbeing in Edwin Chadwick's report on public health (Chadwick 1843). As a result, and starting in London, urban churchyards were systematically closed, subsequent to an act of parliament, the 1855 Burial Grounds Act. This, and the need for unconsecrated grounds for Nonconformist funerals and burials, contributed to the establishment of cemetery companies and new burial grounds on the edge of English towns. Many of these went bankrupt, but the new form of burial was established and today most inhumations take place in large municipal burial grounds, crematoria or natural cemeteries, on the edges of the urban environment.

1. Archaeology and exhumation

This history is mirrored in the history of Sheffield's burial space. It has a large number of historic burial grounds from hospitals to the cramped, overcrowded medieval parish churchyards. It also has large open areas associated with the new nineteenth-century churches built on the edges of towns, the private cemeteries of Nonconformists and the planned open areas of mid to late nineteenth-century garden or general cemeteries. The city contains a good cross-section of sites from Britain's industrial past and shows their current survival rate. For this reason it can be used as a example of what was and is happening across Britain and further afield. As with many of the burial grounds in Britain's cities, Sheffield's cemeteries have been threatened by the expansion of modern life and the spread of population. For this reason a detailed list of cemeteries within the central, historic area of modern Sheffield is given here, to show how and when these sites were reduced, developed or simply lost. Chronological markers allow a comparison with the growth of Sheffield as outlined above (see Fig. 2 for site location). The fifteen burial grounds are listed alphabetically with a brief background and, more importantly, a description of their state of survival today.

A catalogue of Sheffield cemeteries

Broad Lane Quaker Cemetery
This Quaker cemetery is located twice on Fig. 2 because its exact location is unknown. Hunter (1869: 303) mentions a 'large meeting house and burial ground near Bank Street'; however, the Sheffield City Archive holds records of burials from 1740-1854 and 1863-1926 for a site listed as Broad Lane Quaker Cemetery. Leader (1875) places the cemetery down Broad Lane behind 'a high and substantial wall', although he suggests that 'Few persons of the present generation will be aware of that spot having been a Cemetery' (Leader 1875: 196). The first closure date of c. 1854 suggests that it may have closed by order of the Burial Grounds Act, so there may have

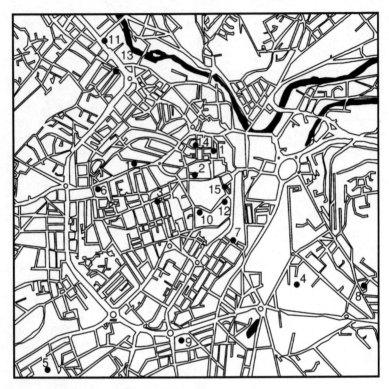

Fig. 2. A plan of modern Sheffield showing the location of fifteen historic cemetery sites within the central area. Many of these sites have been developed and cemeteries can no longer be found at these locations.

1 Broad Lane Quaker Cemetery   9 St Mary's
2 Sheffield Cathedral   10 St Paul's
3 Carver Street Methodist Chapel   11 Infirmary Cemetery
4 Cholera Burial Ground   12 Upper Chapel
5 General Cemetery   13 St Philip's
6 St George's   14 Queen Street Chapel
7 Howard Street Congregational Church   15 Nether Chapel
8 St John's Park

been two separate sites. However, what is clear is that this site, or sites, are no longer present, and were removed at some point after 1875 – probably after 1926 during the early twentieth-century expansion of industrial Sheffield.

Carver Street Methodist Chapel

Carver Street Methodist Chapel sits just off West Street, the route of the Super Tram between Sheffield University and Sheffield Cathedral. Sheffield City Archives hold records from 1806-1855. Some of the graves from this site extended across modern West Street and Rockingham Lane and burials were disturbed in advance of the 1993 Super Tram project (Sayer & Symonds 2004: 56). In 1999 further work was conducted by ARCUS (Archaeological Research and Consultancy at the University of Sheffield) to allow the construction of an external beer cellar by Walkabout Inns. Here, 101 individuals were excavated from 47 grave cuts (McIntyre & Willmott 2003; Sayer & Symonds 2004: 57).

Cholera Burial Ground

In 1832 an Asiatic Cholera epidemic hit Sheffield; its victims, numbering 402, were buried just off Norfolk Road. A monument was erected to commemorate the people who died; this was removed in the early 1990s as it was deemed dangerous following a lightning strike. In November 2006 the restoration of the monument that lies near this burial ground was awarded the 2005-2006 Marsh Award for restoration in public sculpture (Sheffield Hallam University 2009). The burial ground has not, to the author's knowledge, been exhumed and remains an important space and landmark in Sheffield's landscape.

General Cemetery

Sheffield's General Cemetery was opened in 1836 and Sheffield City Archives hold records for Nonconformist burials from 1836-1978 and Anglican burials from 1850-1978 where the majority of burials took place after the 1855 Burial Grounds Act. In the late 1980s some of the Anglican grave stones were cleared to make way for a park area, but public outcry prevented any further disturbance.

Howard Street Congregational Church
The Congregational Church was built in 1787 and Sheffield City Archives hold records for burials from 1795-1840 and 1852-1872: it records just 63 inhumations. In 1966 the building became Howard Street Club and the gravestones were removed, although no mention is made of the burials, suggesting they are still present (Wheeler 1999).

Infirmary Cemetery
The infirmary, named Sheffield General Infirmary, was established in 1793 and was closed in 1980. Its cemetery was removed in 1993 with the construction of the Super Tram along Infirmary Road. The extent and nature of the site is unknown and it is unclear if there are any remaining graves, although this was probably a substantial site suggesting parts of it still remain.

Queen Street Chapel
Queen Street Chapel closed in 1967 when the congregation joined with Nether Chapel (Pitchforth 2004b). The graveyard, which Hunter (1869) records as containing 439 individuals, was closed in 1855. It was probably cleared in 1970 when the gravestones were recorded. The stones were removed and the chapel was demolished. The stones recorded burials between 1787 and 1852 (Wheeler 1999).

Nether Chapel
Nether (lower) Chapel was established in 1715 in Chapel Walk after a split within the Upper Chapel congregation. Manning (1900) lists a number of people who were buried in the chapel's yard. Three chapel buildings have been built on this site which now backs onto a branch of Marks & Spencer (Hey 1998: 86). A survey of 105 gravestone inscriptions was taken in 1965 before the last chapel was built up against Chapel Walk, and so covers

most of the historic graveyard. There are no burial registers for Nether Chapel, although burial stopped in 1855 (Wheeler 1999).

St George's Church
St George's church was opened in 1825, having been constructed under the 1818 Million Act. The cemetery was partially closed in 1855 after the Burial Grounds Act although Sheffield City Archives hold records for burials between 1830 and 1899. Some of the churchyard was cleared in 1962 to make way for a vestry hall (Wheeler 1999). The church is currently owned by the University of Sheffield and is used as a lecture theatre.

St John's Park
St John's Park is a Million Act church, constructed in 1836. Sheffield City Archives have records for burials during the period 1840-1924. The graveyard was closed in 1867, although burials continued until 1884 after which time only three burials took place. Much of this cemetery has disappeared under the road extensions of the 1960s, although there is a complete record of the gravestones which were cleared to make way for the growth of Sheffield (Wheeler 1999).

St Mary's Church
St Mary's is another Million Act church. It was consecrated in the 1830s, at which point its cemetery covered a massive three acres (Hunter 1869). Sheffield City Archives hold records for 1830-1908 but the majority of burials were made before 1880. Most of the cemetery was cleared between 1956 and 1961 to make way for the ring road.

St Paul's Church
St Paul's church opened in 1740. Burial registers exist for the period 1743-1855, and it is believed to have contained some 8,000 burials. It was demolished in 1938 to make way for a Town Hall extension. The outbreak of war in 1939 meant that

this planned extension was never constructed and the area was laid out instead as a garden. This garden was first called St Paul's Garden and then renamed the Peace Gardens. It was believed that all the burials had been removed in 1938, which itself was a local scandal – with witnesses to the 'robbing of the cemetery'. The exhumed burials were reburied in a single mass grave at Abbey Lane cemetery, but at the commencement of development for the 'Heart of the City' project in 1997 human remains were encountered and removed by a clearance company. Limited archaeological involvement was allowed by the clearance company and only thirteen fully articulated individuals were recorded out of the *c.* 150 removed (Belford & Witkin 2000; Sayer & Symonds 2004: 56-7).

St Philip's Cemetery

All that is left of St Philip's cemetery are two gravestones lying next to a park bench in the middle of a traffic island along Infirmary Road. Like the other nineteenth-century churches in Sheffield, this was a Million Act church (Hunter 1869) and the one-acre cemetery went out of use around 1855 when the Burial Grounds Act came into effect. St Philip's church then established Wardsend cemetery in 1857, which was consecrated around 1859. The church was bombed during World War II and stood derelict from 1940 onwards; its parish was amalgamated with St Anne's in 1941 (Pitchforth 2004a). The cemetery was cleared and the remains moved to Wardsend to allow the Infirmary Road widening scheme and the construction of the Super Tram in 1993. Given the size of the cemetery it is probable that some graves remain at this site.

Sheffield Cathedral

Sheffield Cathedral, SS Peter and Paul, has stood in the centre of Sheffield since 1100 and there was probably a Saxon church here before that date. The present church has been rebuilt and extended a number of times, as was Church Street which was extended into the cemetery in 1785, 1866 and 1891 (Vickers 1978). The cemetery was closed in 1855 because of the Burial

Fig. 3. Sheffield Cathedral in 1793; at the time this was Sheffield parish church. The illustration highlights the extent of the cemetery as it existed at the end of the nineteenth century. The gravestones are lying down, although this is probably the local tradition (compare with Fig. 6).

Grounds Act and the monuments may have been flat from as early as 1793 (Hey 1998: 84, see Fig. 3). Burial records exist for the years 1560-1855.

Further to the eighteenth- and nineteenth-century road extensions more recent development projects have encroached on the cemetery. In 1993 an area to the front of the cemetery was excavated by a clearance company to make room for the Super Tram stop (Sayer & Symonds 2004: 56). It is estimated that some 400 bodies were removed (Draper 1993: 8). In 1999 AR-CUS conducted a small-scale archaeological investigation to determine the nature of remains within the site: three grave cuts were excavated and ten individuals identified, and the remains were seen to have been interred just below the surface of the ground, almost directly below grave markers (Sayer 2001). Further work was carried out between 2004 and 2006 with a total of 511 individuals from 100 graves being excavated (O'Neill et al. 2007; Mahoney-Swales et al. forthcoming).

Upper Chapel

Upper Chapel was established in 1700 and has records for 1717-1858 (Baker 2008; Mahoney-Swales et al. forthcoming). An archaeological watching brief was conducted by ARCUS in 2006-7 as four graves had been disturbed by construction work. Previous development on the site took place in 1848 and 1866 and may have disturbed underlying burials; a complete record of the burials overlain by a 1900 extension was taken as well as of gravestones still standing at that point (Manning 1900: 172, 184). Records exist for 160 burials (from 1812-1836, Manning 1900: 184) although Hunter (1869) suggests that over 480 had taken place. This discrepancy may be the unintentional result of the changing nature of the burial provision allowed to Nonconformists during the nineteenth century (see Sayer forthcoming) and if there are more than 160 burials it may be because Nonconformist burials were not always formally recorded.

The Sheffield cemeteries in context

It is evident that all the cemeteries in the centre of Sheffield have been affected by modern development in one way or another. The Cholera Burial Ground and the General Cemetery are the only two which have had their monuments altered but without any underlying clearance, and interestingly both are within parks, protected because they provide green space for Sheffield's modern population and not because they are important burial grounds. Howard Street Congregational Church may never have been expanded and is one of the smallest burial grounds in Sheffield but now there is no physical evidence of the cemetery above ground since the commemorative monuments have been removed.

Just three cemeteries – Nether Chapel, Upper Chapel and St George's – have received limited clearance as a result of religious building extension work, or in the case of Nether

Chapel, several complete rebuilds. This leaves nine sites that have suffered extensive clearance programmes at the hands of city developers (Broad Lane Quaker Cemetery, St Paul's, Queen Street Chapel), or city infrastructure projects, specifically road and tram building (Infirmary Cemetery, St Philip's, St Mary's, St John's Park, Carver Street Methodist Chapel, Sheffield Cathedral). Essentially, of the 18 different development projects identified, four were initiated by religious organisations (including the cathedral extensions), three by private development, and 11 were a result of civic infrastructure projects. Only four out of the total have undergone archaeological intervention; one of these was voluntary and another did not have its post-excavation costs met.

This paints quite a bleak picture. However, it stresses once more the link between prosperity through development and the scale of historical cemetery removal that takes place in today's planned urban environment. This area of archaeology has only recently been recognised by both planners and archaeologists in the UK as potentially significant and has been surrounded by conflict and compromise over the last two decades. Chapters 2 and 3 briefly describe similar conflicts affecting medieval cemeteries that took place earlier in the history of archaeology underlining the point that this debate is as much about the growth of a new industry and an academic discipline as it is about the relationship between today's living and yesterday's dead.

Archaeology and cemetery exhumation

Just like other areas of the construction industry, there are rules that cemetery clearance practitioners have to follow in order to receive a licence to exhume bodies. These rules were outlined in the 1857 Burial Act for cemeteries whose use had not changed. The 1981 Disused Burial Grounds Amendment Act was designed to cover cemeteries that had been closed after 1855 but which were still cemeteries. These regulations were primarily designed so that exhumation projects would not cause offence to the public, rather than as a means to regulate modern archaeology, which at that time did not exist. In a nineteenth-century legal case in which the defendant was tried for grave-robbing, a hypothetical position was discussed by the prosecution counsel. To disturb the 'Druids who had been buried on Salisbury Plain' would not be indictable under common law as they were not 'in such a state that their removal would be a shock to our moral feeling' (*R v Jacobson* [1880], Simon Mays, personal communication, 28 Jan 2009). Today, with the growth of special interest groups, such an argument may not be as compelling, but this case does demonstrate that burial law was not intended to cover archaeological exhumation. Even though many prehistoric cemeteries have been excavated with a licence, this was not strictly necessary. Indeed, even the exhumation at Carver Street, Sheffield, which was conducted on a site where a nineteenth-century cemetery once stood, did not strictly need a licence. The reason for this was that, even though there was a historic cemetery surrounding the chapel, much of which remained, the developed area had been converted into a car park. Its use had therefore changed and that area was no longer a cemetery – and so not covered by the rules. However, this is a somewhat grey area, and quite rightly the excavators applied for, and received, a licence (see Chapter 2).

This ambiguity concerning what was and what was not a cemetery, and to which sites the acts applied, was compounded by silence on the part of the licence-issuing authority. Until 2007 the Home Office was responsible for issuing licences for the removal of human remains; but the responsibility for enforcing the rules of the licence on practitioners was not their concern. When I wrote to the Home Office to clarify this point the reply indicated that it was the local constabulary who were responsible. Conversely, the police, when questioned about this, pointed back to the Home Office (see Sayer & Symonds, 2004: 56). It is perhaps for this reason that the two important rules outlined in the law (2a and 2b) on the treatment of remains with due care and attention to decency, and the screening of remains from the public gaze, have been broken on numerous occasions by commercial exhumation companies.

1. Archaeology and exhumation

One such case involves the exhumation of human remains at Sheffield Cathedral in 1992-3, which saw public outrage at the clearance company's disregard for the regulations. Clear sight-lines existed into the work area and office workers witnessed the processes of exhumation (Sayer & Symonds 2004: 56). Despite this, the public who raised these concerns, and the paper which reported them (Sheffield's *Star*) were not aware of the details of legal regulation of cemetery clearance. Thus this breach of the law was never formally reported and no prosecution was brought against the clearance company. The Super Tram spokesperson claimed that the work was entirely within the official guidelines and that if the 400 or so bodies within the site had been excavated by archaeologists the work would have taken ten years – a situation incompatible with the 13-week deadline for the project (Dawes 1993b, also see Chapter 3, which explores the law further). This was not an isolated event or an unfamiliar situation to archaeologists in the 1990s, as testified by letters published in *British Archaeology* (e.g. Morris 1994).

In 1990 the framework of British archaeology changed completely with the advent of Planning Policy Guidance note 16 (*archaeology and heritage*) (PPG 16). This guidance meant that most development taking place within Britain required some level of archaeological intervention. There are, however, some exceptions, and the Sheffield Super Tram case is one of them. Even though the work took place after the advent of PPG 16, it followed a House of Commons Select Committee on Transport 1990 report and a subsequent act of parliament for the tram works. As a result no formal requirements were placed on the work or the archaeology belonging to the nineteenth-century town. Post-medieval archaeology was still in its infancy and the Cathedral archaeologists were not made aware of the development project and so had not informed the Cathedral of the archaeological potential in cemetery exhumation. Had the Cathedral stop not been in such a highly visible spot and associated with a high profile building this whole episode might have gone unnoticed, as for example happened at the

37

nineteenth-century infirmary cemetery at about the same time.

Later work at St Paul's (Sheffield) in 1997 included archaeological investigation alongside the operations of the cemetery clearance company: a collaboration agreed by the clearance company and not imposed by the council who had the contradictory responsibilities of both regulating and paying for the work (Sayer & Symonds 2004: 57). The archaeologists were allowed to excavate 16 individuals, 13 fully articulated, before finally having to leave because of pressure to clear the area. In 1999 archaeological work was carried out at Carver Street Methodist Chapel (Sheffield) by archaeologists who had overall responsibility for the project. Unfortunately this positive change did not accompany a transformation in developer attitudes and no post-excavation costs for the assessment or processing of the 101 remains, or their associated coffins, ever materialised.

Fortunately, during the late 1980s and early 1990s a number of sites were investigated under better conditions; these include Spitalfields in London (Reeve & Adams 1993; Molleson & Cox 1993) which has proven to be of international importance through its study of existing death/burial records as compared with skeletal remains in order to determine the accuracy of modern osteoarchaeological ageing techniques. However, many skeletal assemblages from cemetery sites of this date were investigated 'by accident,' where the intention had initially been to examine medieval or earlier remains – for example the St Nicholas project in Sevenoaks (Boyle & Kevill 1998). Many projects like St Nicholas, Sevenoaks and also St Nicholas, Bathampton (Cox 1998); St Augustine-the-Less, Bristol (Boore, 1998); St Bride's Church, Fleet Street, the Quaker burial ground in Bath (Stock, 1998); and London Road, Kingston upon Thames (Bashford & Pollard, 1998) were done with little or no funding. However, these projects highlighted the archaeological potential of post-medieval cemeteries and laid the foundations for archaeological research into nineteenth-century remains. As a consequence publications for these sites were realised (Harding 1998; Reeve 1998; Bell & Lee-Thorp 1998; and White 1998).

From the late 1990s onwards the situation seemed to improve, and in a number of notable cases archaeologists were given the responsibility for the large-scale excavation of hundreds of inhumations without the presence of clearance companies. For example, excavations at St Martin's Church, Birmingham, recorded 857 remains, and a local official from the council was present to ensure the conditions of the Home Office licence were met (Brickley et al. 2006: 25). Additionally the developers placed the archaeologists under pressure to publish before the opening of the shopping centre, so publicly drawing attention to their sensitivity to historical issues. However, projects of this size are not common and most crypt clearances and graveyard exhumations have been conducted by archaeologists and clearance companies in tandem. Oxford Archaeology Unit is one of the most active participants in this type of collaboration, exhuming a number of cemeteries and crypts in conjunction with British Graveyard Services (BGS), formerly Necropolis. Sites worked in this way include St Bartholomew's, in 1999 (Boyle 2004); and more recently St George's Crypt Bloomsbury; Vancouver Centre, King's Lynn; and St Luke's, Islington (see Sayer 2009).

On a similar scale to the St Martin's project was the clearance that took place in the extension to the Old St Pancras churchyard at King's Cross, conducted by Gifford's, Pre-Construct Archaeology (PCA) and the Channel Tunnel Rail Link (CTRL). This exhumation saw the stratigraphic recording of 83 inhumations, completed in 2002, in conjunction with a watching brief (where an archaeologist, or small team, was present to record what was uncovered by the developers) that was seriously limited by the conditions of works, for example the simultaneous development of many different elements of the station (Emery 2006). The excavation of this site involved an agreement with the developers to allow full recording of at least some remains. Unfortunately this venture stands as a total contrast to St Martin's, as in December 2002 the archaeological work was suspended and the field team removed from site as a result of developer pressure. However, archaeologists pushed the developers into negotiations and were as a result able to return to work in February 2003 (Sayer 2009; see Chapter 3 below).

The St Pancras case demonstrates how archaeologists made an important stand to protect the heritage of the nation; in particular they were attempting to highlight the significance to archaeology of nineteenth-century remains that had for many years been regarded as of no historic or scientific interest. There are some similarities between Sheffield Cathedral and St Pancras, in that the development work was not subject to the usual planning constraints, having been authorised by an act of parliament (the CTRL Act 1996, *Rescue News*, 2003). Unlike work that had taken place ten years earlier in Sheffield, archaeologists in these two cases were involved from the start and developers' attempts to deny the cultural and historic value of the site by preventing archaeological work therefore failed.

Despite the more positive archaeological environment within which development work now takes place, the process surrounding the exhumation of post-medieval cemeteries remains unresolved, although their cultural and scientific value has at least now been recognised. Archaeological involvement in post-medieval cemeteries is increasingly common, as is the publication of their findings (e.g. Boston et al. 2009; Miles et al. 2008; Miles, White & Tankard 2008; Brickley et al. 2006)

Discussion

Many of the issues raised in this chapter hinge on the relationship between the living and the dead, but also highlight other questions as fundamental as 'what is archaeology?' The contrasting sites of Carver Street Methodist Chapel, Sheffield Cathedral's Super Tram project and St Pancras are useful cases for developing this last question.

Carver Street Methodist Chapel involved the exhumation of

1. Archaeology and exhumation

just over 100 bodies from the footings of a beer cellar. Unsurprisingly, during the course of the excavation, much discussion of an ethical nature was generated. Nineteenth-century Methodists followed a strict doctrine of abstinence from worldly sin. As a result they did not as a rule drink alcohol and indeed many preached against it. Among those individuals who were buried at Carver Street not one would have approved of their chapel being converted into a student bar or sports pub. This prevailing attitude is evidenced in the planning conditions which led to the construction of the external beer cellar: there was an ordinance on the site's development dating back to the time it was used as a chapel disallowing the storage of alcohol within the building, hence the need for the construction of an external storage unit. The developers calculated that it would be easier, and presumably cheaper, to employ archaeologists to excavate a space in the cemetery which would allow for the lawful avoidance of the ordinance that would otherwise prevent the storage of alcohol in the former chapel. This was directly against the wishes of the building's former occupants (although it had not been owned by the Methodist Church for quite some time) and the exhumation of the cemetery was against the spirit of the ordinance, which remains on that site today.

Urban development is inevitable and in some cases also desirable. Both the Super Tram and St Pancras projects had a different underlying purpose: the construction of regionally or internationally significant transport links which would directly affect the lives of tens of thousands or hundreds of thousands of people. Both projects were conducted under acts of parliament and were directly or indirectly paid for by the British taxpayer. The Super Tram was part of a Sheffield-wide transport system that connected many outlying parts of the city to the centre and provided an accessible form of public transport. Although it did indirectly replace an abolished but cheaper bus system, the tram line extended to the newly constructed Meadow Hall shopping centre and so assisted in the general economic recovery that Sheffield experienced in the late 1990s and early 2000s. The whole St Pancras redevelopment project won the

Mayor's Award for Excellence in Planning in 2008 (RPS 2009) and was part of a £2 billion redevelopment project within the station including the renovation of its iconic hotel. The King's Cross area around St Pancras was previously rundown and economically deprived and the redevelopment put it at the heart of a communications network which links London with the north of Britain as well as directly to Paris and Brussels via Eurostar. Life and employment in the area have undergone a considerable and positive transformation.

Even with recent legal changes (see Chapter 2) cemetery exhumation remains very much a part of modern life. The pressure to develop – indeed, the need to develop – urban spaces to precipitate economic growth is a modern reality. The ethical question presented here then is not *whether* archaeologists should excavate post-medieval cemeteries, but *how* they should excavate post-medieval cemeteries – and which ones?

The situation in the 1990s which resulted in archaeological contractors carrying out voluntary work to safeguard the heritage of a town undermines the whole concept of commercially-funded archaeology. However, in this context it was understandable; in the 1980s and 1990s post-medieval archaeology was just developing, as medieval archaeology had been in the previous decades (Gerrard 2003), and it needed to demonstrate that it was an essential part of modern commercial archaeology. This was evident across all sites, not just cemeteries but also urban sites and farms. But it was among cemetery sites that the greatest tensions were created, which still affect commercial archaeology, although less frequently now.

Readers of this book will be aware of what the study of human remains can reveal about the past. For example: individual health, population health, cause of death, diet, lifestyle, attitudes towards the body, religious belief, identity, gender, social relationships and social divisions (see e.g. Roberts 2009; Sayer & Williams 2009). However, the ambiguity over the exact meaning of Burial law and its enforcement tells us something else. Post-medieval burial grounds, like the Victorian garden cemeteries found on the edge of many towns, have been largely forgotten in legal and planning systems. Their grave-stones rot and ivy grows over them. One of the reasons for this is that the legal system was developed when many of these sites were in use, or indeed new. The dead who built our towns are less important than the living who now occupy them. A well-informed study of the recent past and its physical remains can and does contribute to the planning process. What is needed is a stronger understanding of the patterns of development. For example, where cemetery clearance is concerned there are two types of development: (1) civic projects of local, national or international importance, and (2) those initiated for personal or business success. If De Baets (2004) is correct and the dead do have rights, then these have to be considered against our modern concerns and needs and so must be taken into account during the planning process. For instance, it would seem more appropriate for the ordinance preventing the storage of alcohol at Carver Street Chapel to have been lifted than for the developers to engage in an excavation project to get round it, even if it would have been slightly more expensive. This is a type of mitigation strategy, which is not uncommon in other parts of the construction and planning processes. As we shall see in Chapter 3, if the chapel had been a disused Jewish synagogue there would have been no question at all of allowing the exhumation of its private cemetery, as the Jewish community believe in the sanctity of the dead body. However, this is a process which needs to be debated alongside the creation of a new legal framework at the centre of the planning process, not by archaeologists as lone protesters.

The second issue that needs to be readdressed is the practice of archaeological exhumation itself. The screening of cemetery sites as outlined in the law is designed to protect the public against offence, but not all of the public want to be protected. It is modern cemeteries and fleshed remains that are most likely to cause this offence, with the exception of specific cases where other ethical concerns arise. Indeed, it was modern sites that the law was designed to protect the public from when it was passed in the late nineteenth century, and so this particular caveat should be applied only to modern sites. I'm not suggesting that archaeologists remove the hoarding that customarily surrounds cemetery projects completely, but that they consider its removal for those who wish to pass through and see what happens on the inside. It seems paradoxical to screen off the excavation of historic skeletons from the public but to display others in museums or at exhibitions such as the successful *Skeletons, London's Buried Bones* at the Wellcome Collection in 2008. Many of these skeletons come from nineteenth-century cemeteries like those discussed in this chapter. It is perhaps for this reason that cemetery projects often arouse mixed feelings in the public; indeed, it was not the failure of the screens that upset the public at Sheffield Cathedral, it was what they saw going on behind them.

By contrast, elsewhere the heritage sector is pushing for public involvement, access to archaeology through education, community participation and publications which reach as many people as possible. There has been a similar debate within medical literature surrounding public involvement in post-mortem body alteration. Walter (2008) argues that medical autopsies would benefit from selective public viewing, for where a process is hidden it engenders suspicion. Cremation practitioners have benefited enormously from a policy of openness: the opportunity for the public to go behind the scenes and witness the procedures means that trust is high in this post-mortem industry. Likewise if archaeologists are truly ethical in their approach to the excavation of human remains then they should have no qualms about shedding the secretiveness manifest in the physical barrier that separates them from the rest of the community. After all, human skeletons are one of the reasons many people get involved in archaeology, and the study of skeletal remains is one of the clearest impressions that the public have of what archaeology is. Indeed, the excavation of human remains is an emotionally powerful way to explore the human experience, the human condition and human stories, which is after all one of the central purposes of archaeology and something that the discipline should be trying to share.

Archaeology, heritage and British burial law

Introduction

The novelist and poet Thomas Hardy, while an architecture student in the 1860s, was responsible for supervising the exhumation of the cemetery at Old St Pancras, London. The works were being carried out to allow the insertion of the underground tunnel and structural support for the overland railway line. This type of experience affects many archaeologists today (Kirk & Start 1999), and it had a similarly profound effect on Hardy: it was during this time that he wrote the poem 'Neutral Tones', reflecting his persistent problems in relating to women. His later poems 'The Levelled Churchyard' and 'Ah, Are you Digging on My Grave' may have been directly influenced by his experience at St Pancras (Banerjee 2006). His primary responsibilities at St Pancras seem to have been to ensure the ethical treatment of the remains, whose exhumation was conducted behind a 'high hoarding'. As a result he may have been among the first people responsible for enforcing the rules of the 1857 Burial Act and ensuring that exhumation was conducted in the proper manner. Certainly he was there at the request of the architect Arthur Bloomfield, who represented the Bishop of London (Emery 2006).

Although this responsibility may have been required in the nineteenth century, the provision of an officer to oversee the ethical exhumation of human remains has been enforced only occasionally under the more recent Home Office guardianship of that law, as we saw in Chapter 1. However, the issuer of licences for the exhumation of human remains changed in 2008, passing to the Ministry of Justice from the Home Office. The Ministry of Justice initially refused to issue archaeologists with licences, stating that archaeology was covered by common law. This caused confusion and archaeological agents put pressure on the Ministry to change its position.

Burial law was never intended to govern the behaviour of archaeologists, but it is part of a suite of laws that affect burial archaeology, exhumation, skeletal analysis and the display of human remains. This chapter looks at burial law, common law and the Human Tissue Act, and describes cases to which they have applied. There are other laws that affect burial, including the 1984 Anatomy Act and a church faculty of the Ordinary which affects consecrated ground, but these rarely apply to archaeology. The Anne Mowbray reburial, described later in this chapter, is a case study dating from the 1960s, used here to help explain why archaeologists believed they required a licence, and why in 2008 they requested to be covered by that same law even though in its more recent, and more literal, interpretation it specifies the destruction of important scientific remains. The focus here is on the interaction between archaeology and the law rather than on providing advice on the law itself, which can be easily found in the Act on the government website or in guidance documents.

The reinterpretation of British burial law

In 2008 there was a change to the interpretation of the legislation governing the removal of human remains in Britain. The 1981 Disused Burial Grounds Amendment Act still applied to the exhumation of the recently dead and the exhumation of burial grounds still in use or whose use has not changed. However, the reinterpretation meant that the Burial Act of 1857 now covered most archaeological remains and the need for a licence was more likely to be enforced.

The legal change revolves around a reinterpretation of the law as applied to archaeological work by a new authority, the

Ministry of Justice. This change was part of wider reforms to the laws governing the disposal of the dead in modern society. It was initiated with the stated intention of applying one set of rules to burial, cemetery management and exhumation and so simplifying the complex legal needs of these processes. However, there were some teething problems during the transition of administrative duties from the Home Office to the Ministry of Justice, when it failed to issue licences to archaeologists for the removal of human remains. The programme was also inconsistent in that the Ministry of Justice issued some licences with the legal requirement to rebury the remains within just two months, a rule which had previously been applied to exhumation companies that had no scientific interest in the bodies they handled, and so did not need to clean and prepare bones for investigation. As a result, the Institute for Archaeologists (IfA), Council for British Archaeology (CBA) and English Heritage approached the Ministry of Justice to clarify the situation and put forward the case for archaeological work to be allowed to continue and not hold up ongoing construction projects.

The failure to issue licences caused some confusion: in an article in the *Observer* the paper's science editor, Robin McKie, indicated that the new restrictions meant that licences would not be issued for some excavations, which would severely hamper archaeological research in Britain (McKie 2008). McKie also reported from his interview with David Miles, chief archaeological adviser to English Heritage, that the Ministry of Justice would, according to the 1981 law, apply a two-month reburial restriction on human remains. Two days later an article appeared in *The Press* (Small, 2008), a York newspaper, in which Mike Hayworth of the CBA called for the Ministry of Justice to clarify the situation as soon as possible. In response the Ministry of Justice indicated that common law applied to archaeological excavation, not the burial laws. Archaeologists, however, were adamant that the burial laws should apply to them since they had been operating under them and applying for licences for some years (see Garrett-Frost 1992). However, English common law prescribes what you cannot do, not what you can. This means that the reinterpretation of the burial laws would not have hampered archaeological exhumation at all, but would rather have meant that a licence to remove human remains was in fact no longer needed (provided the archaeologists were not working within an existing cemetery). Without the need for a licence archaeological projects would also not have been affected by the restrictions of that licence.

In April 2008 the IfA posted a written response from the Ministry of Justice (2008) clarifying that archaeological work should be conducted as usual, and that it would, as requested, consider archaeology under the law, as it did not wish to prevent

> otherwise lawful and legitimate activities, such as archaeological examination of human remains, to proceed without the constraints of legislation not designed to deal with such issues (point 3, Ministry of Justice 2008).

The Ministry clarified that under the 1857 Burial Act archaeologists would have two years to re-inter human remains, and that extensions could be applied for in special circumstances. It also indicated that it was reviewing the case for application to be made to store remains in museums or churches under a second stage of the reform to this legislation. Cemeteries that have passed out of use are still covered by the 1981 amendment unless their use has changed (such as the extension to Old St Pancras churchyard, London, for example, which was covered by a railway embankment). The problem seems to have been one of interpretation. When the Burial Act was passed it was intended to cover the exhumation of recent cemeteries, which are now in fact historic or post-medieval cemeteries: it was not designed for what archaeologists think of as cemeteries today, i.e. all groups of burials from any period, regardless of cultural affiliation. This is why archaeological exhumation of what the Act identifies as cemeteries is both lawful and legitimate. Despite this, from around 1990 to 2008 archaeological practitioners routinely applied for licences to excavate both historic and more ancient remains where there was no lawful requirement to do so. The reasons for these applications were well expressed in the advice issued to archaeological practitioners by the former Institute of Field Archaeologists (IFA, now the IfA) and the CBA. For example Garrett-Frost (1992), a solicitor of English commerce and industry law, described the burial laws, the penalty for not following them, and how he understood them to apply to archaeology. Under his interpretation all cemetery exhumation work needed to be licensed under that law, and he duly described how archaeologists could apply for one through the Home Office.

However, the reason why archaeologists felt they needed this advice and needed to adhere to this awkward law arose from an earlier context, that of conflict and the experience of archaeological practice in Britain in the 1960s to 1980s. For burial archaeology this situation is well illustrated by the Anne Mowbray case: the exhumation and analysis of the coffin and body of an aristocratic medieval child discovered in London in the mid-1960s.

The Anne Mowbray reburial case

On 11 December 1964 workmen discovered a coffin inside a lost vault that had formally been below the choir of the thirteenth-century Franciscan Nunnery of St Clare Minoresses (or Minories), Aldgate. The coffin was small, at 148 by 28 cm, constructed in lead and formed into an anthropomorphic shape. Unfortunately the workmen who extracted the coffin from the vault wrapped a chain around it and attached the other end to a mechanical digger, so when it was pulled out of the vault it suffered some damage. The workmen informed the police and the press. The police established the age of the remains and realising that they were not of a criminal nature handed them into the care of London Museum's archaeologist (now the Museum of London and the Museum of London's Archaeological Service or MoLas). The coffin was that of a named historical figure, Anne Mowbray, or Anne Duchess of York, daughter and heiress of the Duke of Norfolk. She had died on 19 November

1481, aged just nine – despite which she had been married to the younger of the royal brothers killed in the Tower of London (Molleson 1987; 2002). The coffin was opened on the instructions of the Coroner, and with the approval of the Dean and Chapter of Westminster; also in attendance were the director of the museum and six others, including archaeologists, medical specialists and technical staff operating overhead cameras (Moorhen 2005).

The press reported on the case from the perspective of the interest generated by the accidental discovery of an important medieval aristocrat and a member of the royal family. This, and the damage to the coffin, created bad feeling among Anne's living descendants, the then Lord Mowbray and the Duke of Norfolk, who called for the analysis to be stopped and the remains reburied immediately. This was also reported in the press, as were the questions asked in parliament and the failure of the London Museum archaeologist to inform the Home Office of the discovery of the remains and to acquire a burial licence for their removal. In April 1965 a retrospective licence was granted by the Home Office to the London Museum, but it required that the analytical work be finished by 15 May. It was also granted on the condition that no new work was to be undertaken and stated that the remains should be handed over to the Dean of Westminster by 31 May 1965 to facilitate reburial. It is unlikely that a modern parliament could or would create a series of new conditions for a particular licence as was done in this case (see below for further discussion), but the case raises issues about who owns the past.

The work was completed, the remains handed over, and a private reburial ceremony took place. Anne was stitched into a blue padded lining and returned to her repaired coffin. It was sealed and laid in Westminster Abbey 'on a cloth covered table embroidered with the heraldic insignia of the Tudor royal family and the arms of Westminster Abbey ... . Her slender coffin lay lengthwise on the table surrounded by four gilt candlesticks, and a large processional cross ...' (Watson & White forthcoming: 4). The *Observer* (1965) ran a colour supplement

2. Archaeology, heritage and British burial law

titled 'The world of Lady Anne Mowbray' and the reburial was reported in the *Daily Express*, the *Daily Telegraph*, *The Times* and as far afield as the *New York Times* and the *Chicago Tribune* (all 15 January 1965, with the *New York Times* covering the reburial on 31 May 1966). The media coverage of Anne's story was huge; very few archaeological sites receive media coverage at all, let alone a continuous narrative which runs through the broadsheets and foreign press. From her discovery, through the controversy, and up to the reburial ceremony, Anne had captured the public imagination.

However, the implications of this story are much broader than public interest, and some important questions remain. Did the archaeologists actually need a burial licence? In this case they had not removed the remains themselves but instead received them from the police who consulted the coroner before turning them over. The archaeologists probably believed that they were conducting legitimate research within the law (Collins 1965). Furthermore, the site was not a contemporary burial ground, having been out of use for some time. Indeed the wording of the 1857 Burial Act indicates that it applied to 'any Place of Burial' but the notes in the margin claim that 'Bodies not to be removed from Burial Grounds, save under Faculty, without Licence of Secretary of State' (An Act to amend the Burial Acts 1857: clause 25: 807). This refers specifically to 'Burial Grounds' not to buildings. Furthermore, the implication made by the need for a second Burial Act, passed in 1981, to extend licensing to disused sites, is that the 1857 Act (or the 1884 amendment to that Act) did not apply to disused crypts or burial grounds which had passed out of use. If no burial licence had in fact been needed, the circumstances surrounding the exhumation and reburial of Anne Mowbray were exceptional. Figures with political and economic power used their influence to alter the course of a 'legal and legitimate' exercise and impose a series of questionable additions to the burial licence when it was issued. Watson & White (forthcoming) state that among the aims of the project was a desire:

to enable the London Museum to consult with the authorities on the proper course of action concerning the reburial of Anne's body. Due to the redevelopment of 14-18 St Clare Street she could not be reburied on site.

This suggests that the archaeologists had planned to contact the Home Office, and that they intended to discuss the matter with Anne's descendants if they could be identified. In fact the first Duke of York's line had died out with Anne, and finding surviving relatives would not have been a simple matter. Anne had been lost for nearly 500 years and if her discovery was made today she would still be regarded as one of the most important scientific discoveries of the century.

What makes the Anne Mowbray case important to the history of archaeology is that the attitude of some members of the establishment towards Anne's removal and the archaeological intervention is recorded in the parliamentary records. Hansard records a number of questions raised in parliament, for example:

LORD DERWENT
My Lords, I am sorry to press this matter, but are any of these things that are supposed to have been discovered really of the slightest historical interest? Is the noble Lord aware that this is a public museum controlled by the Government? Is it not about time that the Government stepped in and said that these experiments – and they are little more than that – should stop? (Vanden-Bempde-Johnstone 1965: 182-5)

Despite the conditions placed on the research it was agreed that it had some historical value and that rushing the reinterment of Anne's remains would serve no purpose. Further to this, in 1966 a question was asked concerning when the London Museum's report would be published, since this report was seen as an important part of the process, justifying the archaeological intervention (Mackenzie 1966); at the time the report on Anne's teeth was the only formal publication (Rushton 1965).

2. Archaeology, heritage and British burial law

It is important to remember the context within which the events of the Anne Mowbray case took place, as it is unlikely that they would be repeated today. In the 1960s there was no national policy protecting archaeology and heritage, though this issue was under debate. Indeed, Lord Alport used the Anne Mowbray case to raise the question of the stewardship of archaeology and heritage in the House of Lords (Alport 1965), although actual legislation was not passed until 1990.

Archaeologists working under the system before the 1990 legislation began a protest campaign to protect the future of England's past. The Charitable Trust RESCUE was formed in the early 1970s: this was a pressure group that campaigned for an official source of funds to allow archaeological recording in advance of construction projects (Hunter & Ralston 1993: 34). Archaeologists had to work outside the establishment but it was very important for them that their work be protected and legitimised through proper legislation, so that it would be officially recognised. Their campaign aimed to focus public interest on their efforts to conduct archaeology responsibly, and these efforts eventually led to the passing of PPG16, which safeguarded the industry by forcing developers to pay for archaeology within the structure of the planning process. Within this context medieval archaeology was itself only just emerging as a legitimate area for study or research within the discipline; the Society of Medieval Archaeology had been established in 1957 (Gerrard 2003: 95-131).

The archaeologists of the 1960s did not question their compliance with British burial law; they worked within the regulations that had been imposed on them and halted their research programmes to allow for reburial. The Anne Mowbray case had in fact set a dangerous precedent and any professional archaeologist who had watched these events unfold would have considered it wise to seek either legal advice or a burial licence when they conducted their own excavations of human remains. Despite this, when excavating, prehistoric burials licences were not commonly applied for, and it was not until 1992 that the IfA (then the IFA) published technical paper No. 11 'Archaeology and the Law' (Garrett-Frost 1992: 2) in which it advised that 'it shall not be lawful to remove any body, or the remains of any body, without licence'. However, within that same document, Appendix Four: Scots Law, James Logie observed that the existing case law 'is concerned with human remains which are in areas which were accepted burial places either at the time when the relevant case was decided or at some point prior to that decision' (Logie 1992: 13). Even though this point is based in Scottish law, the same statement could apply equally well to English law. Despite this, the guidance document advised that the removal of human remains from any location, modern, historic or prehistoric, should take place with a licence.

The burial law today

The burial law and its reinterpretation in 2008 was not designed for archaeologists and the need for this reinterpretation was not driven by archaeology. However, the response by archaeologists to the Ministry of Justice's reinterpretation of that law was swift. The national bodies that safeguard heritage and archaeological practice acted responsibly and in unison to make a request for clarification, a situation that could not have taken place in the 1960s as no such bodies existed. However, as an industry, archaeology had simply reacted to the new reinterpretation and had not actively sought to prevent it in the first place – not necessarily appropriate action for a modern profession.

The burial law had been under review for some time. Back in 2001 the House of Commons select committee on the environment, transport and regional affairs resolved to make an inquiry into cemeteries. In parallel with the House of Commons inquiry, the Living Cemetery Project put out consultation literature and English Heritage was included within the list of contributors (Sayer & Symonds 2004: 59). English Heritage, like the other 129 contributors, focused purely on Victorian garden cemeteries and their fabric, with no consideration of buried archaeological remains within many cemeteries and

2. Archaeology, heritage and British burial law

Fig. 4. 'The Dig Issue', a topical cartoon highlighting the plight of the tombless, by Nick Newman. Published in the Sunday Times, © The Times 23/04/2000, reproduced with kind permission of NI Syndication.com.

deconsecrated chapel and churchyard sites (ibid.). In 2004 a further consultation document was put out by the Department of Constitutional Affairs, entitled 'Burial Law and Policy in the 21st Century' (DCA, 2006). There were 383 responses, including those from archaeological officers, Birmingham city archaeologists, English Heritage and the CBA. Only one comment was published (question 23) regarding the potential damage to buried archaeology if deeper graves were cut into modern cemeteries. The issue was not that archaeologists were oblivious to the need for change; the 'Guidance for Best Practice for the Treatment of Human Remains' (Mays, 2005) was drafted by English Heritage and the Church of England at the same time to advise and ensure the ethical and proper treatment of exhumed skeletal material, but it is not a government policy. The actual legal change was in fact driven by the pressures on modern burial space caused by an increasing elderly population and the need to reuse burial sites and graves. This was well summarised in 2000 by an article in the *Sunday Times* with an illustration of a skeleton selling the 'Dig Issue' and uttering the line 'Help the tombless!' (Leake 2000; see Fig. 4). Arguably the requirement to rebury Christian remains exhumed from churchyards described by the Guidance document issued by English Heritage simply adds to the pressure on burial space.

Importantly, because the reinterpretation of the legal position by the Ministry of Justice was not driven by heritage issues, heritage professionals did not pick up on it and realise its wider implications. Despite the government's stated intention to have one law governing burial, archaeologists and their representatives failed to recognise that a change to this law would affect the licences that they had been working under. In other words the legal framework changed without adequate representation of the heritage issues that it affected.

The reinterpretation of burial law places all archaeological cemetery excavations under the 1857 Burial Act, and so requires their reburial within two years. This in itself is not a significant change: a burial licence issued before the change by the Home Office would have stated that:

C) The remains, if of sufficient scientific interest, shall be examined by **** ****** a suitably qualified person under the arrangements of **** ******.

D) The remains shall, if of sufficient scientific interest, be conveyed to a museum for archival storage under the arrangements of the above, or they shall be conveyed to a place where burials may legally take place and be reinterred.

The last section D) specifically requires reburial and presumably when it was drafted its author did not expect entire excavated sections of nineteenth-century cemeteries to be regarded as of sufficient scientific interest to be stored in museums and other archaeological archives. That said, such a requirement may have applied only to cemeteries as understood by the Act of 1857, and so not to the majority of archaeological excavations, particularly those of pre-Christian or prehistoric sites. Where only a limited number of remains has survived, there is a good case for their having 'sufficient scientific interest' to warrant long-term storage to enable a programme of research through archaeological science. Scientific approaches might include isotope investigation, ancient DNA or dating methods, all of which can provide invaluable insights into these individuals and ancient communities. Regardless of this, archaeologists requested that they be reintegrated within the licensing system when excavating any site – not just post-medieval cemeteries – despite the increased vigilance needed in enforcing the requirement for reburial. This effectively means a case has to be made for the scientific value of each skeleton or each cemetery assemblage, no matter how old they are. Such a move may seem difficult to understand: why would scientists seek to classify unique material within a legal category that requires its destruction after a limited period of time when they had the option to work under the common law which does not require reburial?

The answer perhaps lies within the paradigm of protest: the archaeologists involved in the request for legal clarification were heritage professionals, and among their aims was the desire to safeguard archaeology; however, their perception was that excavation had to stop because the removal of human remains was no longer lawful. If it was not legal to remove human remains then the Anne Mowbray case could be repeated, a dangerous situation since the number of projects requiring the removal of human remains has increased substantially since the 1960s. For example, between 1989 and 1999 the annual number of projects involving human remains rose from around 100 to over 600 in the Republic of Ireland because of the increasing need for regeneration and development work (O'Sullivan 2001: 121).

The exhumation and investigation of archaeological skeletal remains is a special category of heritage not covered by heritage laws, which tend to focus on ownership. As such it needs a separate legal framework for its practitioners to operate safely within. Without such a special status anyone, not just 'suitably qualified persons', could conduct the exhumation of ancient human remains for any purpose – scientific or otherwise – and could do so perfectly legally. However, the burial law as it stands was designed for unconsecrated or deconsecrated grounds, and consequently those remains not in consecrated ground and that could never have been in consecrated ground are now affected by a Victorian law which was passed to protect Christian remains from improper exhumation, both by clandestine grave-robbers and by unscrupulous developers. Such a law is inappropriate for dealing with modern scientific interests and developments and redundant for the building trade which is now well regulated by planning requirements. While burial law is needed to ensure that the proper respect is shown to both ancient and modern remains, current legislation is inappropriate for the breadth of tasks that it is now required to cover. Recently the Ministry of Justice has suggested that it may consider allowing human remains over 200 years old to be exhumed without a licence: an implementation being considered for summer 2010 (Tucker 2009).

In Scotland the situation is further complicated since under Scottish law, like German law, the dead body has a right to burial (the right of sepulchre) – a law which originates from a previous historic context. Historic Scotland (2006) regards careful excavation as unlikely to breach this law (which like the English law was designed to prevent the desecration of modern graves); nevertheless archaeologists have to be aware of its conditions, which govern how archaeological projects are established and how remains are treated when they are discovered.

One of the questions not covered by the burial laws is the ownership of exhumed remains: a similar question to who owns our heritage, who owns the past, who controls access to the past and who owns the artefacts that come from it (Carman 2005). Garrett-Frost (1992: 1) outlined further complications for burial archaeology where under English law it is impossible to own human remains. In other countries similar laws apply: for instance in the USA it is illegal to sell human tissue, and responsibility for human remains lies with the landowner (see the Kennewick Man discussion in Chapter 4). The Anne Mowbray case highlights this legal issue over ownership: if her remains had been owned then the question of access and study

would have been based on ownership, not historical heredita-
bility or ancestry. If the London Museum had been in a position
to buy the remains from the landowner, as with a hoard defined
in the Treasure Act, then there would have been a legal basis
for their scientific study. It is therefore important to discuss
who owns human tissue as it has implications for how the
dead are treated, particularly affects what archaeologists do
today, and will almost certainly affect the future of burial
archaeology.

Who owns human tissue?

No discussion of the law and human body parts would be
complete without a brief discussion of the events surrounding
Alder Hey Children's Hospital at the turn of the last century,
especially as there are similar controversies over body parts in
the USA (Andrews & Nelkin 1998). In 1996 parents of a young
girl discovered that a surgeon had retained her heart after a
failed attempt to carry out open heart surgery. The heart was
promptly returned to the parents by the hospital authorities
after a formal request. Because of concerns about this case an
action group was established to raise the profile of similar
cases. In 1999 a public enquiry about child mortality at Bristol
Hospital drew attention to the large number of children's organs retained at Alder Hey Hospital, Liverpool (Redfern et al.
2001: 447-58). In December that year Lord Hunt established
the Alder Hey Inquiry Panel. The subsequent report revealed
the 'systematic stripping' of organs from every child who had a
post-mortem. It also revealed that over 100,000 organs, body
parts and entire bodies of foetuses and still-born babies were
stored by the NHS (Redfern et al. 2001). The families of the
Alder Hey children sued the NHS.

However, it is not the scandal itself that is of interest here, it
is its aftermath. During this period the press reported on the
growing anxiety among medical practitioners that the public
would no longer donate their organs for transplant for fear of a
disingenuous system (Boseley 2000). In 2001 the Royal College

of Pathologists held a symposium at which it was decided to audit institutions that retained human remains, including anatomy museums (Sayer & Symonds 2004: 59). In 2004 the Human Tissue Act was passed to regulate the removal, storage and use of human organs and other tissues for scheduled purposes; this law also covered the regulation of organ donation to ensure informed consent. As a result a statutory authority, the Human Tissue Authority (HTA) was established in 2005 to provide inspection of and licences to institutions that stored human tissue for research, public display and organ transplant. The Human Tissue Act does not apply in Scotland, but a separate law was passed in 2006, the Human Tissue Act Scotland, which granted its ministers the power to request assistance from a UK statutory body (the HTA) in the administration of an ethical framework for the storage, display and transplantation of human tissue. It was designed to link with the UK law. However, there is a key difference between the two laws: the Scottish law is based on the idea of authorisation whereas the English law is based on consent.

Despite these recent events the storage of human remains has long been an area of conflict. In 1997 the artist Anthony-Noel Kelly displayed sculptures prepared from casts he had made of dissected body parts. The rubber sculptures were recognised as made from real remains by Her Majesty's Inspector of Anatomy and the matter was referred to the police. It was discovered that Kelly had paid a trainee lab assistant to help him remove over 40 body parts from the Royal College of Surgeons (Cohen 1997). He also did not have a licence from the Inspector of Anatomy for an anatomical exhibition. The remains were recovered from his garden, his studio and attic. The argument used in his defence was that the Royal College of Surgeons did not treat the remains respectfully.

Anthony-Noel Kelly's actions could be seen as part of a tradition of Renaissance artists who used real cadavers, for example Mantegna, Leonardo, Michelangelo, Caravaggio and Rembrandt, all of whom used dead bodies to study human morphology. However, unlike these artists his intention was to shock as part of a culture that prevails in modern art (Sawday 1997), seen also in Damian Hurst's shark or calf in formaldehyde. Kelly was sentenced to nine months in prison for theft, which implied ownership of the body parts by the Royal College of Surgeons (Sengupta 1998). This story is important because it asks who owns the dead, or their parts. It is impossible to own people in life, which would be tantamount to slavery, but what about after their death? If it is possible to own the dead then what does this say about the rites of the dead, and their relationship to the living?

The legal ownership of the dead is a question which needs to be explored further. Another similar example comes from the Australian High Court, which in 1908 ruled in a case about a two-headed foetus. The foetus had been preserved for display but it was seized by the police. A Mr Dodewood sued for the return of the display item and the court agreed, the Judge stating that:

> when a person has by the lawful exercise of work or skill so dealt with a human body in his lawful possession that it has acquired some attributes differentiating it from a mere corpse awaiting burial, he acquires a right to retain possession of it, at least against any person not entitled to have it delivered to him for the purpose of burial. (Wilkinson & Coleman 2001: 142)

This example raises further questions: for example, is or was an unborn foetus a person, and could its body therefore be regarded as constituting human remains? The case of Anthony-Noel Kelly did at least address the legal question of ownership. After he was found guilty of theft he lodged an appeal, arguing that under British common law it was impossible to be guilty of the theft of body parts because they are incapable of being another's property. The court of appeals judge upheld the original conviction, arguing that:

> as a matter of law there is an exception to the traditional common law rule that 'there is no property in a corpse',

namely that once a human body has undergone a process of skill by a person authorised to perform it, with the object of preserving for the purpose of scientific or medical examination or for the benefit of medical science, it becomes something quite different from an interred corpse. It thereby acquires a usefulness or value. It is capable of becoming property in the usual way and can be stolen. (Wilkinson & Coleman 2001: 142)

The Human Tissue Act does not change legal ownership, it simply licenses the storage and display of human tissue that is less than 100 years old. The Human Tissue Act does not resolve the question of foetal consent for archaeologists; rather the Human Tissue Authority identifies a foetus as the mother's tissue and advises that while this understanding does not extend to babies it is good practice to receive consent from the mother when considering taking tissue from stillborn children and neonatal deaths.

More recently the question of ownership became an issue when in 2009 the Shambles Museum, Newent, Gloucestershire closed down, and its entire collection was put up for auction. The collection included human remains and the event was covered by the national news. A representative of the British Association for Biological Anthropology and Osteoarchaeology (BABAO) phoned the auction company and expressed its concern about the legality of the sale, saying that it was 'considered poor practice and generally unacceptable amongst the museum and heritage sector' (Martin Smith, BABAO, 19 May 2009 email to members). The auctioneer promised to make the owner aware of these issues. After a similar event, members of BABAO contacted the Human Tissue Authority and asked what their position was on the sale of human remains. Its reply indicated that the Human Tissue Act was silent, and it considered that retailers and internet auction companies have their own regulators and standards which apply. Ruth Hughes, a regulation manager, also stated:

2. Archaeology, heritage and British burial law

A key principle on which the Act is based is that all bodies, body parts or tissue should be treated with respect and dignity. The HTA considers that the need to maintain dignity and respect is paramount in the handling of all human bodies and tissue. (Ruth Hughes, 8 June 2008, email reply to BABAO)

Some retailers and auctioneers do have such standards, for example eBay, one of the largest internet auction sites, states that it will not allow the sale of human tissue, skeletons or skulls unless for medical use. This relates to the legality of the situation in the USA and is not an independent ethical stance by the auction company. However, in the UK it seems that one has to prove that human remains have been altered to uphold a conviction for their theft although it is perfectly permissible to profit from their sale. Presumably there is a difference between the sale of medical items or medical teaching aids and skulls that have been altered as cultural artefacts on the one hand, and the sale of human remains for profit on the other. Where they have been altered they become more than human remains and less than human: they become artefacts and as such have a cultural, scientific and economic value. However, this is not the end of the story; even though human remains may be purchased if they are less than 100 years old their new owner must seek a licence from the Human Tissue Authority to store those remains and demonstrate that they are being held in an ethically responsible manner – otherwise they would be in breach of the Human Tissue Act.

In both the Alder Hey and Anthony-Noel Kelly cases, the protagonists were dealing with modern human tissue. They were not stealing archaeological remains, nor were the interpretations of the law or later Human Tissue Act designed to apply to archaeology. However, some of the consequences of these events do affect the heritage community. For a start, the Human Tissue Authority regulates anatomy museums, and the growing awareness of the need for a universal policy for museums led the Department for Culture, Media and Sport to introduce guidance for the storage and display of human remains in museums. Indeed, it is now policy in some Scottish institutions not to display skeletons at all, regardless of their age. Even the common law idea that it is not possible to own skeletal material affects the way people perceive ancient human remains, and it is important to examine the implications of this when considering the burial laws, their reinterpretation and how they apply to archaeology and the Treasure Act.

The ownership of humans and the Treasure Act

This discussion primarily applies to human remains. However, past peoples often included personal effects, grave-goods and burial paraphernalia or coffins in the burial process. Garrett-Frost (1992: 5) regarded the removal of grave-goods as falling under the remit of common law ownership or theft rather than burial law and thought that for burial sites up to and including the medieval period it would rarely be possible to establish the original ownership of such goods. This means that in Britain objects found with bodies of archaeological interest belong to the landowner, whereas the bodies themselves cannot be owned – a situation which may be contrary to the developing principle of storing artefacts and bodies found in one place together (see e.g. Historic Scotland 2006). The 1996 Treasure Act identifies precious metals as treasure and therefore allows museums to raise the funds to purchase these items from the owner (in practice often both the finder and the landowner, where permission was sought by the finder, e.g. a metal detectorist, to search the land). This applies to objects which contain at least ten percent precious metal and which are over 300 years old, or if prehistoric, any base metal object. Any number of precious metal coins or finds of ten or more base metal coins are also covered, provided they are over 300 years old. The Treasure Act also covers all the objects found with material that would be covered by the Treasure Act.

In order to widen the recording of amateur finds beyond the

discovery of precious metal, the heritage community constructed a voluntary programme: the portable antiquities scheme. Objects not covered by the Treasure Act are now routinely reported on a national scale by amateur metal detector users. This provides archaeologists and museums with a good record of the number, type and location of objects and helps not only to identify future sites but also helps to uncover everyday objects which were lost, as opposed to those in the structured deposits that are routinely excavated as part of archaeological intervention. The scheme also legitimises an ancient practice that has never been entirely socially acceptable: *London Labour and the London Poor* (first published in 1851), describes 'mud larks', children forced by poverty to search the Thames foreshore for valuable objects (Neuburg 1985). Looking for objects outside a scholarly tradition has been labelled 'treasure hunting' and associated with the poor or nighthawks who search fields at night without permission and so are little more than thieves. The museum community and finds liaison officers now record objects and return them (assuming they are not treasure) to the finder. Many people keep these as they are interested in the objects and their history, and they enjoy the chance to own the sort of materials that are normally only seen in museums. Unfortunately many people also choose to sell the items they discover.

The internet auction site eBay often has objects found by metal detector users listed among its auctions. Most of these are legitimate finds registered with the portable antiquities scheme where permission was obtained from the landowner. Examples include worn brooches, buckles and pins. However, groups of objects sold as single lots also sometimes appear, such as a recent auction of Anglo-Saxon beads, two cruciform brooches and a buckle, which are strongly suggestive of gravegoods, and this seems less legitimate. At the time of writing (October 2009) there were a number of worn brooches listed, including parts of an early medieval cruciform brooch, a pair of disc brooches, and a pair of identical saucer brooches, which, as pairs, are more likely to have been associated with a female burial than to have been the result of accidental loss.

These items may have been turned over and out of a grave by a plough, or the finder may have dug down to a burial to find the source of the metal signature recognised by the detector without ever seeing bones (some bones do not survive or the digger makes small holes that miss the bones) so their discovery may be entirely legitimate. However, it is also possible that old cemeteries are being used as mines for commercial gain, and with the reinterpretation of the burial law these cemeteries are covered by the laws designed to protect decency. Although the removal of objects is not in breach of the burial laws if human remains are not removed, nevertheless the deliberate removal of objects from burial is covered by common law which can prosecute for the desecration of a cemetery or tomb since ancient cemeteries and modern ones are now both regarded as cemeteries under the burial laws (compare with the situation described in North America in Chapter 4). For instance, you may not steal the coffin fittings from a recently buried coffin, or tip over grave monuments under common law, nor may you dig up burials with the intention of removing objects from them unless a licence has been issued or a Faculty of the Ordinary (of consecrated grounds) has been granted for the removal of specific objects. There is precedent for this need: in 1869 Dante Gabriel Rossetti, artist and poet, applied for and received a Faculty of the Ordinary to recover the manuscripts of poems he had placed in his wife's coffin – the public distaste at this act effectively ended his popular career.

Discussion

British archaeology is still characterised by its past as a protest movement. Many of the current leaders of heritage organisations once fought for the provision of funds to pay for archaeology. This may have contributed to the ill-planned response by heritage organisations to the Ministry of Justice's first refusal to include archaeological exhumation in its reinterpretation of the burial law. Notably, this is not the situation with more overtly heritage issues, such as the redevelopment of Stonehenge or the illicit smuggling of antiquities. In the 1960s the case of Anne Mowbray forced archaeologists to pay attention to the legal and ethical requirements of working with human remains, but archaeologists would be wise to note that laws that are not intended for ancient human remains can nevertheless directly affect how they are treated. The burial law, the ownership question in common law and the Human Tissue Act all affect how skeletal material is perceived, how it is excavated, how it is examined or how it is displayed to the public. Moreover, archaeology has become increasingly popular and politicised. Heritage issues in the UK and further afield, for example in Iraq, are now mentioned in parliament on a regular basis (see Fig. 5). However, with this increased politicisation archaeologists also need to be more politically aware.

The issues surrounding the burial laws remain largely unresolved by practising archaeologists or the custodians of the law.

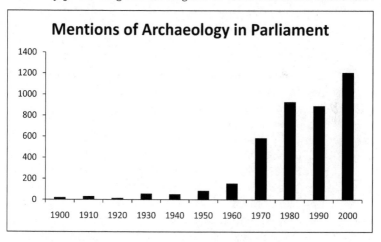

Fig. 5. The number of times archaeology has been mentioned in parliament in the last 100 years by decade. The bar chart shows a dramatic increase between the 1960s and 1980s where archaeology is mentioned around 1,000 times a year in the 1980s and 1990s and over 1,200 times in the 2000s. This information is based on how many times the word archaeology appears in Hansard, the official publication of parliamentary debate and questions.

The odd fit of current laws to archaeology is well demonstrated in the following hypothetical case study: when excavating a Roman town, an event that happens across commercial and academic archaeology every year, a digger is almost certain to come across human skeletal material. There are two types he or she might expect to encounter: (1) disarticulated adult bones, a skull in a pit or ditch, a tooth, or long bone; (2) articulated neonatal or foetal bones in pits or as part of house deposits. So the question is, does the archaeologist need to apply for a licence for the removal of these human remains? These individuals were not buried in a cemetery, or even a burial ground as understood by the law. They were not buried in deconsecrated or even unconsecrated ground, as that type of Christian burial did not exist. Further, is a single skull a burial at all? It is human remains, but is it the deliberate burial of an individual? A neonatal child's body may be a case of infanticide, but it is also possible that it was stillborn and in either case had not been incorporated into society, so was not perceived as human. Even the Human Tissue Act is not clear about the latter point for modern remains so it is unlikely to be resolved for archaeological remains from an ancient period. Indeed, is it appropriate to apply modern sensibilities at all or should the ancient Roman or ancient British attitudes to burial be considered, if it is possible to determine them? In English and Welsh examples it may be better to consider applying a Scottish approach to their excavation based on the Human Tissue Act's central remit – dignity and respect. In Scotland the law is not about permission but about authority, so do archaeologists have the authority to excavate remains rather than permission from the deceased? A final thought: if they were not viewed as human or were not burials then do they need to be reburied? For instance, ancient remains found outside a cemetery or within a structure like a long barrow may not have been considered as disposed of or buried and were simply in storage for processing or later retrieval.

Perhaps future burial archaeologists should work within the premise that once ancient human remains have been preserved and scientifically recorded, and once they have contributed to our understanding of the past, they become valuable scientific objects, capable of being owned by museums or research communities, and that they should therefore be unaffected by the burial law. At the same time they become more than human remains, but less than human beings, just like anatomy specimens in common law. However, as archaeology is primarily the study of past people and human cultures, a move towards dehumanisation within the industry may not sit comfortably with many of its practitioners. Indeed, such a blatantly legally determined and political position would be contrary to the very thing that makes human remains of scientific interest: the fact that they were once people. One thing is clear: the legal position concerning the archaeological excavation of ancient or more modern skeletal material remains unresolved and a single law based on modern cemetery protection is not the answer.

3

Human decency, politics and digging the dead

Introduction

We're digging up all of the graves and we're spitting on
the past.   DiFranco 1998

This line comes from a song entitled *Fuel* by the American folk
singer Ani DiFranco. It was written as a statement about the
archaeological work conducted at New York's African Burial
Ground. The song is a representation not of the excavation
itself but of the protest which surrounded it, in which archaeologists were accused of damaging human bones and of releasing evil. The African-American community wanted not only to
participate but to take charge of the excavation; as a project it
stands in complete contrast to similar excavations in Philadelphia and Maryland where the local community was not excluded from involvement in commercial projects but instead
took part in the initial project design. These cases highlight an
important point: the past matters to communities, but human
remains are also sometimes used as pawns by social or political
movements with broader motivations.

This chapter looks at a number of cases in which exhumation projects attracted public protest from disenfranchised
political or identity groups, and although respect for those
remains is often cited in the ensuing conflict, it is rarely the
underlying motivation for the protests themselves. The bones
do not always matter, it is the past or the use of the past that is
often the main issue. This theme is explored here through the

relationship between living communities and cemetery exhumations, particularly focusing on sites such as Rapparee Cove (Devon), Jewbury (York), Bonn Square (Oxford) and Fromelles (northern France), which have attracted wider interest and been caught up in public protest.

However, conflict with the public has not always been a negative influence on archaeology. It has been used successfully, for instance, in protests about the methods adopted by exhumation companies. By examining the contexts within which individual exhumation projects become the focus of protests, and relating them to the wider issue, it will become clear that there is no single public opinion about archaeological exhumation, nor is it necessarily a particularly sensitive topic. Exhumation can be a sensitive topic, but individual circumstances, politics and the behaviour of archaeological companies all affect the questions concerning the use of our past.

Identity and public protest

America's African diaspora

Native American sites and the repatriation of human remains to the descendants of indigenous communities have dominated discussion of ethics and reburial in the USA. When the Native American Graves Protection and Repatriation Act (NAGPRA 1990) was passed it focused not on disenfranchised communities and the survivors of all groups affected by western colonialism but only on Native Americans, because they had been the main proponents in its creation. Notably the act did not represent African-American burials and so within NAGPRA there was no legal requirement placed on scientists to treat the remains of slave and diaspora communities in any special way (Roberts & McCarthy 1995: 21-2).

The situation for African-American cemeteries was similar to that for Native American ones, so accusations of institutional racism were made alongside allegations of the mistreatment of human remains. However, this impression taken alone would be a misrepresentation of American archaeology. Early on, historic archaeologists operated in partnership with descendant communities. One of the better known, and published, examples of this is a project in the First African Baptist Churchyard in Philadelphia which provided scientific evidence for the lifestyles of the individuals interred within it (Parrington & Roberts 1984). These people must have been among the first free African-American communities in Philadelphia (Angel et al. 1987). This site, Eighth and Vine Street, Philadelphia, and a second site, Tenth and Vine Street, were excavated in partnership with local descendant communities (Roberts & McCarthy 1995). At Eighth and Vine Street burials were first uncovered unexpectedly in 1980 ahead of construction of a commuter train tunnel. The work was stopped and exhumations were undertaken in 1983 and 1984, when 140 bodies, dating between 1825 and 1842, were excavated. A research programme was put together which considered the interests of the decent community as well as those of historical science. A series of tours and impromptu education programmes resulted in an estimated three to four thousand people benefiting directly from this excavation through personal experience (Roberts & McCarthy 1995). The work also included a TV programme entitled *Ground Truth: Archaeology in the City* which Roberts and McCarthy (1995: 27) described as a 'very positive' representation within the media.

From the outset the programme proactively sought reburial, and representatives from the First African Baptist Church arranged for this reburial in plain cardboard containers within five large concrete vaults side-by-side in a large grave-pit (Roberts & McCarthy 1995). For the 1980s this reburial was very forward thinking for archaeologists, and it was the result of the community involvement in the project that allowed such measures to be taken to enable the descendants to show respect for their dead.

In apparent contradiction to the Philadelphia case are the events that surrounded the discovery and renaming of the African Burial Ground in New York. This was uncovered by accident ahead of a federal office building programme. Excavation began in the summer of 1991 and saw the exhumation of 420 burials. However, the research programme was inadequate for the job (La Roche & Blakey 1997) and additionally a large scale and emotional protest by New York's African-American descendant community blighted the project. The protests were so fierce and emotions flowed so freely that the event became immortalised by Ani DiFranco in the independent music scene some seven years after its discovery: 'They were digging a new foundation in Manhattan and they discovered a slave cemetery there, may their souls rest easy now that lynching is frowned upon' (DiFranco 1998).

The protests at Manhattan became particularly heated after protesters, using telephoto lenses, spotted the accidental destruction of several graves by a mechanical digger. A new team, under new terms, was therefore put together, including archaeologists who had been involved in the two Philadelphia projects – their role was to manage public interaction (La Roche & Blakey 1997). However, in spite of the publication of newsletters and other interactive outreach programmes, the damage had been done, and African-American groups became increasingly frustrated. Subsequently the cemetery excavation was halted by government intervention; an African American congressman acting on the advice of New York City's first African American mayor stopped the excavation works (Harrington 1993). The absence of proper funding provisions for post-excavation analysis was revealed and the remains were removed to Howard University, Washington, which has historically been an all-black institution. They were welcomed with a spiritual ceremony and the analysis of the excavated remains was headed by physical anthropologists from that university (La Roche & Blakey 1997). After more lobbying, President George Bush Snr signed Public Law 102-393 ordering the federal authorities to stop the construction and released $3 million for a museum, memorial and the reburial of the remains following scientific investigation (Skeates 2000: 30).

The African Burial Ground is an interesting case as it is a case in which archaeologists were vilified by an outraged local community who had not been consulted before the work commenced (Harrington 1993). The effective and sophisticated African-American lobby at city, state, and national levels demonstrates how much the archaeologists and construction company had misjudged the importance that the African-American community placed on their desire and ability to interpret their own past and not to receive it second-hand. Archaeologists attempted to demonstrate that they were respectful and 'sensitive' to the descendant communities' needs but these efforts fell short because they came after the defamation of white middle-class involvement. The archaeologists had already been cast in the role of destroyers of the truth and partners in yet another social injustice (Carver 2003: 2-13). Indeed, there were people who believed the archaeologists were releasing evil through their work in the cemetery (Harrington 1993). Even though opinions were divided within the African-American community about exactly what should be done, one thing was clear, the 'African Americans sought control, not sympathy' (La Roche & Blakey 1997: 96). For example, the site was first marked on historic maps as 'Negroes Burying Ground' but was renamed by the protest movement the 'African Burial Ground', a title which mirrored the terminology that the descendant community used to describe itself (La Roche & Blakey 1997: 94). Furthermore, it was widely believed that this project was just another attempt by a white ruling majority to deny the North's participation in slavery and the African American historical involvement in constructing New York (Beaudry 2009). This protest, and the opinions held at the time of the exhumation, were particular to this context and deeply political.

A similar project at the Freedman's cemetery, Dallas, Texas, was conducted ahead of a road expansion scheme. The project took place between 1991 and 1994 and collected over a thousand inhumations interred at the end of the nineteenth century. As in Philadelphia, local and state-wide interest groups were involved, as were the distant relatives of the interred. These groups included: Black Dallas Remembered, Inc. (the local African American historical society) and the

Temple Emanuel Cemetery Association (Davison 2004: 6). Although contemporary with the project in New York this excavation did not receive the same level of protest. One of the reasons for this was probably because the interest groups were consulted early in the process and were allowed to put an embargo on intrusive scientific investigation. Despite this successful collaboration, the project was criticised by the Howard University physical anthropologists for the embargo and the underanalysis of the skeletal remains before reburial (Blakey 2001: 414). However, even with the apparent destruction of important scientific data, the Dallas project provided important evidence about the treatment of the African Americans. For example, there is evidence to suggest that African-American bodies were illegally taken for use as medical cadavers (Davidson 2007). This case, the Philadelphia project and by contrast the African Burial Ground demonstrate that partnering with the African-American communities can help to ease the political tensions over the ownership of the past and modern racial tensions (Roberts and McCarthy 1995). As further evidence, the excavators of a second slave cemetery discovered in the north, in Portsmouth, New Hampshire, not only involved the local community in the project but asked them what specific research questions they would like answers to (Goldman 2006). This successful project and the other three cemetery projects discussed make it clear that it was probably not the actual removal of human remains that was of greatest concern, despite the horror and spiritual beliefs expressed at the time: more important was the political question of who has control over the interpretations of the past.

Britain's slave cemetery
A remarkably similar case is still ongoing in the UK. Rapparee Cove was excavated in the 1990s, and although its origin has not yet been resolved it has been the centre of much interest from Britain's own African diaspora and the population of the Caribbean island of St Lucia.

An interesting research excavation on the rocky north coast

of Devon, designed to rescue bones from an eroding cliff, is the only contested slave burial site in the British Isles and instantly became the focus of international controversy. The excavation was organised by an historian with a particular interest in north Devon and was carried out in collaboration with an archaeologist from the University of Bristol. In 1997 the London politician Bernie Grant visited the beach site to call for the reburial and commemoration of the Africans uncovered there (Gibbs 1997). He and a similar-minded party of people visited the site because it was suggested that the remains were African prisoners of war who may have been destined for the slave markets in Bristol. The bodies may have come from a British ship, the *London,* which sank in 1796 off Ilfracombe while on the way to the Bristol Channel; the ship possibly carried prisoners from St Lucia, French prisoners and gold (Barrow 1998).

Bernie Grant led the ceremony of remembrance at the site in 1997 (Smith 2006: 4) which was one of the most widely reported events organised by the UK branch of the Africa Reparations Movement. However, this was not the end of the matter and the discovery was brought up in parliament on 16 June 1999 by the MP Harry Cohen who asked the secretary of state about the status of these remains; he also asked after the progress of research. The question was repeated on 26 October (Cohen 1999a, 1999b). In 2001 St Lucia's representatives stated that they were going to approach Britain formally to discuss the repatriation of the bones (Whitney 2001). By this time the National Slavery Memorial Day campaigning group had registered their interest in the discovery and identification of the remains so that they could be repatriated (Whitney 2001).

No research results were forthcoming, and in 2007 the *Guardian* reported that requests for further information ahead of the bicentenary of the abolition of slavery had been 'fobbed off' by the archaeologists (Morris & Constable 2007). While there is not, as yet, a publication of archaeological results, archaeologists claimed to have contacted St Lucia to explain that the origin of the remains could not be identified but that

3. Human decency, politics and digging the dead

they were probably not the remains of Africans (Morris & Constable 2007). Moreover, they argued that, based on diet, the remains were probably French soldiers, or locals from the Devon beach (Whitney 2001). However, the results of this analysis have not been peer-reviewed or scrutinised by the wider scientific community, which is essential given the relative infancy of skeletal isotope studies and the absence of any study looking specifically at the diet of a ship's crew.

What is interesting about this case is the political situation; the story of how these bones got to the beach in Devon is interpreted differently by the three separate interest or identity groups. The St Lucians see them as freedom fighters, national heroes, who were fighting the British to avoid re-enslavement during the Napoleonic upheavals that saw many Caribbean islands achieve independence from their colonial masters, if only temporarily. The African Repatriation Movement (ARM 2009) has campaigned for reparations to be made for the slave trade, and so its interpretation of the Rapparee Cove remains focused on a story about a slave ship. According to them the ship sank causing the deaths of all the occupants who drowned on their way to incarceration and slave markets, and ARM's early involvement in this project meant that it was used as a high profile rallying symbol for the slave trade reparation cause in the UK (the UK branch of ARM was founded in 1993). The archaeologists, however, argue that there is no way to link these remains directly with the lost ship, and suggest that the remains could be those of local fisherman, farmers or French soldiers, and so until their origin is proven there is no justification for repatriation. Despite all these conflicting and controversial opinions no research project has been established to resolve the question of who was buried at Rapparee Cove. The myths surrounding this site are exemplified in a book written by a professional historian who inadvertently misrepresents the slavery element of this site, claiming the identification of 'manacled human remains' (Smith 2006: 4), based on the first news reports in *The Times* which actually state that 'Yesterday the first iron fetters were discovered in the shale' (Constable & Farrington 1997). Indeed, archaeologists (Horton, personal communication) have suggested that these 'manacles' may come from a different context to that of the bones and may even be part of a nineteenth-century bathing machine.

The reluctance of the archaeologists to publish or make available any of the detailed scientific information produced from this site may be internally fuelled but adds to the controversy and mystery. By not actively involving Britain's African community or other international interest groups in their post-excavation findings, archaeologists have simply alienated and disempowered those communities who are already seriously underrepresented in British archaeology. The three different interpretations have become so independent and the accusations so emotional that it no longer matters whether Rapparee Cove was a slave cemetery or not – it will always be surrounded by questions and suspicions.

The importance of involving multiple-interest groups in archaeological projects and their interpretation is not just relevant to individual excavations; it could have an impact on the future of the discipline. UK archaeologists have not learned the lessons of New York and as a result are in danger of following in the footsteps of a more recent exhumation crisis surrounding the excavation of an early colonial cemetery from Prestwich Street, Cape Town, South Africa. Here the archaeologists insisted that science was more important than the public reaction (Beaudry 2009). The direct result of this attitude was an increasing separation between archaeologists and the local community within South Africa. Deep mistrust was focused on archaeologists who appeared disengaged with contemporary society and the broader public (Shepherd 2007).

However, Rapparee is not alone in having generated controversy in British archaeology. Other minority groups in the UK have expressed concern over archaeological exhumation projects: most notably the British Jewish community over an excavation which took place in York.

3. Human decency, politics and digging the dead

Archaeology and religious conflict

Jewbury, York

The circumstances surrounding the exhumation of a twelfth/thirteenth-century medieval cemetery at Jewbury, York, are reasonably well known and have been one of the few burial ethics case studies cited from the UK in recent history (e.g. see Parker Pearson 1999: 179-80; Bergquist 2001: 187; Payne 2009). However, the project provides useful insights into the theme of this book, so it is worth revisiting the events in more detail.

In 1980 a proposal was put forward to develop a plot of land on the bank of the River Foss, land which had been regarded as the traditional burial ground of the Jewish community, as shown by medieval records. By the time archaeological involvement was sought, the IFA (now the IfA) had published a set of guidelines which recommended that archaeologists take into account the legitimate concerns of groups whose material remains may be subject to archaeological investigation (IFA 1981: 1). Bearing in mind this concern, the York Archaeological Trust approached York's Chief Rabbi, who in turn informed the Trust and the City Council of the religious importance that the Jewish community placed on the sanctity of burial. He approved of a plan to identify the extent and nature of the burials and the limits of the cemetery, so that the proposed development would avoid causing too much damage. As a result, archaeological involvement continued (the events of this case took place ten years before PPG 16, so archaeological participation was not yet a planning requirement). The Chief Rabbi strongly suggested that even if it was impossible to avoid the development of the land, the cemetery's occupants should be respectfully excavated and reinterred elsewhere (Addeyman 1994).

The evaluation to locate the cemetery went ahead and bodies were uncovered. They were oriented north-south in wooden coffins, many held together with iron nails. The results were conveyed to the two stakeholder groups: the developer, J Sainsbury plc, and the Chief Rabbi. The Rabbi was surprised by the findings: it is, or was, a widely-held belief that Jewish coffins should be held together with wooden pegs not nails, and that they should be interred on a west-east orientation facing Jerusalem. He was also surprised that there were no Jewish gravestones. After the evaluation, the developers agreed there was no way to avoid building on the cemetery and at the same time allow for the construction of a car park facility for the supermarket. The matter was referred to the Chief Rabbi's court, the *Beth Din*, for further consideration. This religious court ruled that there was no conclusive proof that the cemetery was Jewish. However, because a few individuals may have been Jewish, and in the wider interests of human decency, they advised that the remains be excavated before construction work could take place and suggested those remains should be reburied promptly. It has been suggested that this was a view taken by the *Beth Din* to avoid a contest between scientific and religious discourses (Bergquist 2001: 187). The 1981 Burial Act had just been passed so there was already perceived to be a legal responsibility to excavate respectfully and rebury any skeletons within a year. With the religious issue settled and the legal situation clear, excavation work went ahead between January and May 1983, including the beginning of full post-excavation recording and skeletal assessment (Addeyman 1994).

During the course of the work, the *Guardian* newspaper reported on the project, making it clear that the site was being developed. A number of members of the public made requests for more information from York City Council, and an orthodox group from the Jewish College at Gateshead presented arguments to the Chief Rabbi that the remains were almost certainly from the medieval Jewish community (Parker Pearson 1999: 180; Bergquist 2001: 187). The Rabbi wrote to the Home Office and York Archaeological Trust, who then outlined the archaeological importance of the site, stating that it is one of only ten Jewish medieval cemeteries in England and that scientific investigation would be invaluable to the understanding of Jewish history and the place of Jews in medieval society. The Rabbi responded:

3. Human decency, politics and digging the dead

Whatever the scientific and historical loss, I hope you and the general public will appreciate our paramount concern for the reverence due to mortal remains which once bore the incorruptible hallmark of the divine image, and which we believe, have an inalienable right to stay undisturbed. We are convinced that the dignity shown to human remains, even centuries after death, could contribute more than any scientific inquiry to the advancement of human civilisation and the enhancement of the respect in which human beings hold each other. (Addeyman 1994: 300)

The Home Office responded by immediately requesting the cessation of skeletal investigations and requiring the reburial of the remains by December 1993. The skeletal collection was handed over to the supervision of the Manchester *Beth Din* and reburial took place on Sunday 8 July 1984 in a plot adjacent to the site which had been provided by J Sainsbury plc.

This is not a textbook case where a stakeholder community denied or withdrew permission for archaeological excavation (*contra* Rahtz 1991: 46-9); unlike with the New York slave cemetery, the archaeologists had approached the representatives of the Jewish religion to open a dialogue and to discuss their requirements. A religious court had found the remains unlikely to be Jewish and a burial licence had been applied for and received, but an internal conflict within the religious community led to the legal prevention of further work. Moreover, the skeletal analysis of 496 individuals was being paid for by the Science and Engineering Research Council to facilitate a speedy process and allow reburial to take place within the time limit imposed by the new licence, issued under the 1981 Burial Act (Addeyman 1994: 299). However, in this case a licence to remove human remains issued by the proper authorities, after due process and after all stakeholders had been consulted, did not provide any legal protection for the archaeologists at all. Legally, did the Home Office in fact have the right to revoke the licence without notice and after retrospective decision-making by a stakeholder community?

The skeletal remains were not undisturbed and could not have remained undisturbed because of the supermarket construction. The law required that they be treated with dignity and that they be reburied before the end of May 1984. In terms of 'the respect in which human beings hold each other' in western culture there is no higher form of respect than to show an interest in someone's life and to try to understand their personhood and achievements and to tell their story. However, this case seems not to be about respect for the dead at all but respect for the living Jewish community in the UK, and like other examples from this book, the Jewish community's attitude was based on the idea that the bones were being interfered with in some inexplicable but 'scientific' way. The principal result of this controversy was that York Archaeological Trust found it hard to secure funds for the publication of the project, and the volume was only finally made available in 1994, ten years after the excavation had taken place.

One of the main dissimilarities between the Jewbury case and the slave and African Burial Grounds discussed above is that the individuals involved, the Jewish community, were not actually a descendant community and so may have had quite different views about the body, burial and the afterlife than were represented in the beliefs of the medieval community that was uncovered. This can be seen in the differing orientation of burials and the different methods used to secure their coffins. However, this community's objections to the archaeological work were heeded by the licensing authority despite an existing licence, and archaeological work was stopped. Notwithstanding this result, there is no doubt that the York Archaeological Trust behaved appropriately in involving a stakeholder group from the beginning of the project, whatever the internal strife that existed within that community.

Three Christian case studies
Other religious groups offer different cases studies. The Sheffield Methodists were consulted at the beginning of the Carver Street project and expressed an interest in the results of the

excavation but placed no caveats on the project itself. Similarly, modern Quakers (the Religious Society of Friends) were consulted at the beginning of the Quaker burial ground project, London Road, Kingston-upon-Thames (Bashford & Pollard 1998). They showed great interest in the excavation and readily gave their permission so that it could go ahead, although they asked that the remains be cremated and then returned to them for reburial. However, the society also gave permission for palaeopathological specimens of particular scientific interest to be retained under the supervision of a suitable archaeological institution (Bashford & Pollard 1998:163).

These last two examples, Carver Street and London Road, were post-medieval burial grounds, but the St Albans Abbey exhumation is a good example of a project where medieval bodies, of similar date to the Jewbury burials, were excavated, examined and reburied without conflict. In 1978 the medieval remains of the builders of St Albans Abbey (abbots and named historical figures including the father of Pope Adrian IV) were removed from what had become the Anglican Cathedral in St Albans to allow for the construction of a new chapter house. The remains were examined by archaeologists, returned and reburied under the high altar with a new memorial slab to mark the spot; to honour the occasion the Cardinal Archbishop of Westminster, a Benedictine, presided over the service, and the office of Vespers of the Dead was sung around the country by Benedictine monks (Bergquist 2001: 187-9).

Despite the results of the Jewbury case, protest and protesters against exhumations have not always been at odds with archaeological interests. Objections over the scene witnessed at the Sheffield Cathedral exhumation seem to have benefited archaeology, making local planners more aware of archaeological interests in advance of later projects. Indeed, protest surrounding the events at King's Cross St Pancras directly benefited that archaeological project while complaints may actually have had little or nothing to do with archaeology at all. Some of these sites will be outlined in the next section.

Politics, protest and exhumation in the UK

Sheffield Cathedral

A good example of public protest focused on a pre-PPG 16 exhumation can be seen in a discussion of the exhumation of human remains at Sheffield Cathedral's Super Tram stop which took place during 1992 and 1993. As we noted in Chapter 1, this project saw public outrage at the clearance company's perceived disregard for decency (Sayer & Symonds 2004: 56). A ten-foot high security screen was erected around the site, but despite this effort office workers in local high-rise buildings could see into the exhumation site and witnessed labourers allegedly throwing remains into black plastic bags. It is also widely rumoured that some of those bags were found at the local tip, although this has never been proven. Complaints were received by the local paper who reported that:

> Shocked office workers are overlooking the exhumation of bodies from the historic Sheffield Cathedral graveyard. (Dawes, 1993a: 1)

Despite the public's focus on decency and the treatment of human remains, the discussion in the paper focused on the visibility of the work (see Fig. 6), while the treatment of remains was dismissed as 'within guidelines' (Dawes, 1993b). Unfortunately the public who raised these concerns and the paper which reported them (Sheffield's *Star*) were unaware of the details of the operating licence required to remove human remains. Thus neither a prosecution for breach of decency nor one for the failure to secure sidelines was ever brought. The requirement for decency in the licence can be seen as clearly breached in this case, not because of the use of plastic bags to move skeletal remains, which is still a practice widespread among commercial clearance companies, but because the decency which the regulations refer to is about not causing offence or distress amongst the living. It was designed to avoid just this type of scandal, and so the company, Kenyon Emergency Services, was in breach of this regulation. As it

Fig. 6. Sheffield Cathedral in 1993 during the Super Tram construction works. This photo was taken for *The Star* to show the failure of sight lines and consequently the visibility of the exhumation area from surrounding offices (Dawes 1993a). Reproduced with kind permission of Sheffield Newspapers Ltd.

happens the company continued their work from within a fo- rensic-style tent, so they must have recognised a need to con- duct the remaining project more carefully.

Sheffield archaeologists wrote to the paper and made a strong case for archaeological involvement in this project (Sayer & Symonds 2004), and while this intervention did not happen immediately the human decency and historical science arguments seem to have eventually prevailed. Following the partially successful St Paul's collaboration (see Chapter 1) all other exhumations in Sheffield city centre have involved ar- chaeological excavation.

King's Cross St Pancras

In London, exhumation at St Pancras burial ground for construc- tion of the new Eurostar terminus – St Pancras International – was undertaken between 2002 and 2003. As the archaeological contractor appointed by Rail Link Engineering, Gifford's sub-contracted Pre-Construct Archaeology (PCA) to provide a field-work team who would work alongside British Graveyard Services, a cemetery clearance company. The Museum of London Specialist Services (MoLSS) were engaged to undertake post-excavation analyses. In November 2002, the archaeological work, which had up until that point included stratigraphic excavation of 83 inhumations, was suspended and the field team removed from the site as a result of programme pressure (Sayer 2009; Emery 2006).

The *Evening Standard* reported on the situation:

> More than 1,000 graves are being destroyed by contractors building the St Pancras Channel Tunnel terminal in what government advisers have called 'a desecration' and 'an outrage against human dignity'. Archaeologists excavating human remains from up to 2,000 graves have been suddenly ordered off the site of the Camley Street Cemetery at St Pancras as Channel Tunnel Rail Link company (CTRL) prepares to start digging them out. They had completed work on only about 100 graves. The experts wanted to identify the graves and then contact living relatives of the dead. They also believed they could gather vital information which would help build up a picture of life in London during the Industrial Revolution. (Smith 2002)

After this report the Church of England, English Heritage, the Council for British Archaeology (CBA), and RESCUE interceded alongside Gifford and the Museum of London to put forward the case for continuing archaeological involvement. Following renegotiation of the terms of the intervention the archaeologists returned to work in January 2003. By the end of the project they had recorded over 1,400 inhumations and recovered over 1,100 coffin fittings (including some 150 breast-plates). The skeletal remains were subsequently reburied (Emery 2006). The development work at St Pancras was not subject to the usual planning controls, having been passed by an Act of

Parliament (CTRL Act 1996). However, unlike the Sheffield Cathedral case, archaeologists were involved from the beginning of the project and a successful integrated approach to archaeological recording prevailed, with good relations between the clearance company and Gifford/PCA staff. The archaeological community had made an important stand to protect the heritage of the nation (Sayer 2009) but significantly, and as was reported in the *Evening Standard*, they had couched that protest in terms of both scientific interest and the need for 'human dignity' or respect for the human remains they encountered.

Two sites in Oxford

Despite the success of archaeologists in presenting themselves as the ethical, or respectful, choice at St Pancras they have not always been seen in this way in Britain, just as in North America and elsewhere. Two recent archaeological projects in Oxford highlight a contrasting situation that can be seen with cemetery excavations.

Bonn Square in Oxford city centre was the site of recent media attention when the county council's plans to remodel the square were met by local protest. In a situation dubbed 'the siege of Bonn Square' by the *Oxford Mail* (2008a), protesters tried to stop the felling of a tree before the square was redeveloped. The protesters were finally removed on 14 January 2008 when one of them came down from the tree. The site was secured, a barrier was erected and archaeological work started on what was the site of a medieval and a later post-medieval church and churchyard, which had been covered by the paved square. The project focused on the fabric of the remains, including the brick shafts, gravestones and coffins, all of which were later reinterred on site. The majority of remains in the churchyard were not disturbed by development work as there was no substantial construction and many remains were left *in situ*. Where skeletons were disturbed they were reburied elsewhere on the same site (Oxford Archaeology 2008). However, protest continued on a smaller scale outside the barrier and after the trees were removed attention refocused on the exhumation of the historic cemetery. According to the newspaper one local claimed that he had many ancestors interred within the site:

> The work clearly needs to be handled in a sensitive way. We have already had an angry call from a resident to say that we are digging up about 90 of his ancestors. (French 2008)

In addition, according to Oxford Archaeology staff, the archaeologists were subject to verbal abuse by protesters. Some of the feelings evoked by this project can be seen on the local news website (*Oxford Mail* 2008b) which indicates a general ignorance about the archaeological process and the frequency of this type of work across the UK, and the need for a hoarding to screen off the work from general view. Indeed, at the time of viewing the last post on the website claimed that the archaeologists had been involved in a secret conspiracy to keep the truth hidden.

By contrast, and about the same time, a similar archaeological project was undertaken during road improvements around the Plain Roundabout, on the other side of Oxford. This was the site of Old St Clement's Churchyard. The work did not attract media interest or local protest. Indeed, the St Clement's Parish newsletter cheerfully invited the residents of St Clement's to participate in the reburial that took place shortly afterwards. The remains were reinterred in the New St Clement's churchyard and a memorial will be erected to commemorate the individuals reburied.

Prittlewell

Despite the protests at Bonn Square, local politics and public feeling can also use archaeology for its own ends, as was seen at Prittlewell, Southend. When a seventh-century furnished 'princely' burial was discovered there protesters felt that their cause, to prevent a road widening scheme, had been enhanced (Pitts 2006). After the remains had been removed and it was announced that the road scheme would go ahead these protesters did not react negatively against the archaeologists but instead saw the site as an important historic landmark and sacred place. Eco-protester Adrian Harris describes the location of protest tunnels designed to disrupt the road building scheme:

> Any digging that has gone on ... has taken place in an area that has already been compromised by other previous work .... We didn't even dig a compost toilet on site because of the archaeology. We found a way of having an extensive tunnel network in a way that doesn't disturb the archaeology. (Pitts 2006)

For these protesters the discovery of this burial and the surrounding cemetery was a positive addition to their campaign, just as it was for the protesters at Bonn Square in Oxford, but rather than blaming the archaeological intervention they used the discovery to bolster the protest with eco-pagans actively avoiding damage to any further buried remains, skeletal material or otherwise. However, reaction may depend to some extent on what is perceived to be archaeology and the age and nature of the site. For example if the remains of Boudicca, the Iron Age Queen of the Iceni, had been discovered under the platform extension at King's Cross International (for a discussion of this possibility see Sarre 2002) rather than more recent individuals, the developers might have been all too happy to have archaeological assistance and media attention focused on the discovery.

Fromelles, northern France
The importance of the date, or perhaps more importantly the events that particular archaeological remains are associated with, is highlighted by a more recent project with some emotive issues for modern Australians. In 2009 Oxford Archaeology conducted an exhumation at Fromelles in northern France. The site at Fromelles was the result of a catastrophic military action of the First World War. This action was intended, at

least in part, to provide a distraction from another action 80 kilometres to the south: the Battle of the Somme. On 19 and 20 July 1916 two Allied divisions, consisting of Australian and British infantry, attacked a German stronghold on two flanks. The resulting battle saw the greatest loss of Australian lives in one 24-hour period and the near destruction of both battalions (McMullin 2006). The eight mass graves that were the focus of this modern archaeological project were dug by German forces after they had recaptured the territory occupied, albeit briefly, by the Allies. The bodies of the Australians and British were interred 2 kilometres behind enemy lines (Oxford Archaeology 2009). The graves were unfortunately missed during the imme- diate post-war burial campaigns and only rediscovered by Glasgow University Archaeological Research Department in 2008. After this discovery the Australian Government asked for tenders from an archaeological contractor who would exca- vate the graves so that the bodies could be identified and reburied. The job was won by Oxford Archaeology.

The controversy surrounding this site was reported in the Australian media in 2009 when the exhumation was under way. The headlines read: 'Cheap choice derails graves project' (*Brisbane Times* and *Sydney Morning Herald*, Totaro 2009), 'Rudd denies archaeologists cut corners in Fromelles exhuma- tion' (Live News 2009), 'Fromelles remains safe in our hands: Rudd' (ABC News, Rogers 2009) and 'British, Australian sol- diers in Fromelles, France, in limbo' (*Herald-Sun* 2009). More detail was provided by the *Sydney Morning Herald* which had led with the story:

> The ambitious project to exhume, identify and reinter 400 British and Australian soldiers forgotten for 90 years in a mass grave in a field in France is in crisis after the Department of Defence chose a cut-price, commercial ar- chaeological firm. Last week the *Herald* was invited to visit the site as an 'exclusive' project to document re- trieval of a body and its passage from the mass grave to the mortuary and anthropological and DNA process. But

only 24 hours after the invitation was issued, it was withdrawn without explanation. (Totaro 2009)

Oxford Archaeology did not come out of this story well, being depicted as slow and incompetent, having achieved next to nothing in the time already allowed. However, most of the negativity seems to have resulted from a cancelled 'exclusive' press opportunity and not from the actual method of exhumation. Oxford Archaeology had discovered empty grave-trenches early on, delaying the recovery of human remains. Closer inspection of the press coverage also suggest that it was not the project itself that was the target; indeed competitive tendering in commercial archaeology means many companies could be described as 'cut-price'. Rather this was an opportunity to sling a journalistic shot at Kevin Rudd, Prime Minister of Australia, and his Department of Defence, using the emotive power of the mass graves as a vehicle for that shot. Indeed, it is he who is cited in defence of the project by livenews.com and ABC News. The project could be used in this overtly political way because it struck a chord with living individuals and relatives of the dead, many of whom had been asked for their memories and DNA by the Australian government so that the bodies in the graves could be identified and reburied in a war grave cemetery, as opposed to a mass grave (Oxford Archaeology 2009). Indeed, archaeologists seem to have been unaware of the significant impact of this project on people's lives and it was only after the negative press coverage implied secretiveness that they put the details of the methodology and progress on their website (Oxford Archaeology 2009).

The secrecy and non-disclosure at the African Burial Ground, Rapparee and the hoarding at Bonn Square, all perceived as evidence of clandestine behaviour by archaeologists, created suspicion and distrust on the part of outside interest groups and in turn led to accusations of disrespectful behaviour, incompetence or conspiracy. Human remains can be used as a powerful emotional tool, and the groups with a personal relationship or interest in them extend beyond scientific and historical enquiry.

Discussion

This chapter has looked at a number of archaeological projects which were subject to outside protest. It has highlighted some case-specific aspects of the relationship between the public and exhumation projects. However, what is particularly interesting is when these are considered as a group, because in all of the projects discussed, there is only one example where the protesters' interests were actually focused on the treatment of the human remains. This was at Jewbury, where the Chief Rabbi had no interest at all in the survival of historical or scientific data but only in the decent treatment of the dead who had once been the image of God. However, even this case is similar to the others in that it was a group of orthodox student rabbis who forced the Chief Rabbi to overturn his own court's ruling and require the archaeologists to stop their analysis. Indeed, this political element is apparent throughout the case studies. At Bonn Square the protesters had been more interested in the removal of a tree and in preventing development work, just as they had been at Prittelwell, but at these two sites the protesters made different decisions based on the nature of the particular remains, and their physical or temporal relationship to them, i.e. named relative or ancient ancestor. The protesters then either used the archaeological work as a further point of protest or as extra support for their campaign. In these cases it is not the bones that matter, it is what the bones mean that is important.

In the examples selected for discussion many of the arguments that occurred at the time of the cemetery exhumations were about the treatment of remains; however, what has seemed more important when taking wider perspective is the point about access and interpretation. The past holds meaning for the people of the present, and where projects focus on disenfranchised social and political groups they will desire an involvement in that project, but more specifically in its interpretation. When this has been part of the archaeological project design, investigations have not been hampered by protest but instead have attracted much more positive media interest, even if the request for only non-intrusive analysis has occasionally to be accepted. The best examples are the contradictions evident in the African Burial Ground and slave cemeteries as well as Prestwich Street, South Africa, where the separation of white scientists and African people was further compounded by the separation of science and culture. The same is true of Britain's slave cemetery, where the archaeologists involved in the project seemed oblivious to the interests of community groups, instead regarding it as an archaeological curiosity or scientific question.

The involvement of stakeholder groups at different stages of a project is becoming more common in the US, and if archaeology is going to survive in its current form in South Africa it will need to do the same. However, in the UK this lesson still needs to be learned. It does not seem to be just a question of racial identity, as it may have appeared in the US and South Africa, rather in all of these places protests seem focused on access to the past and its interpretation. When archaeologists do not involve the interested public they are accused of incompetence or secrecy and conspiracy, as at Bonn Square and Fromelles. Despite this, had circumstances been different the relationship between protesters and archaeologists at Bonn Square may still have been difficult because the protest itself was not about archaeology but about control of Oxford's public spaces and trees. However, much of the tension and personal abuse could have been reduced if the archaeologists had removed the stigma they attracted as frontline facilitators of the development.

It is not enough for archaeology to run to the public every time there is a problem, for example the legal change described in the previous chapters, the exhumation at Sheffield Cathedral, or the development of King's Cross St Pancras. At the same time archaeology has to give something back at a local and national level or it may not always be an ethical option. Public opinion is not a simple thing and does not apply to every site or every exhumation in the same way, even where circumstances are similar. However, the nature of public interest may be at its most receptive when archaeologists give something back and participate in community archaeology. Archaeology, as opposed to grave clearance, is an ethical alternative but when it is hidden away behind hoardings or science then it engenders suspicion. British archaeology, like South African archaeology, should learn from the lessons of New York's African Burial Ground project and incorporate public involvement in commercial projects as a matter of project design and in conjunction with museum and planning officials. If it does not there will be more examples of Rapparee, Bonn Square and Fromelles in British archaeology and across the world, and archaeologists would be in danger of distancing themselves from the general public as a result.

4

Display, repatriation and respect for the dead

Introduction

The repatriation of human remains from British museums has been the primary focus of several recent studies (e.g. Fforde 2004, Jenkins 2008). However, and quite interestingly, archaeological textbooks like Roberts (2009) focus very heavily on the repatriation debate in the New World, particularly North America, New Zealand and Australia (Roberts 2009: 17-19). They often discuss recent developments in religious repatriation like the issues raised by the Pagans HAD (Honouring the Ancient Dead) within this context. Other articles take those individual claims out of context, such as discussing HAD without its broader Pagan background (e.g. Moshenska 2009). This is not to say that British universities and textbooks should not partake in either of these debates; they are very important because they affect how remains are perceived across the world, by researchers and campaigners, as was highlighted by Roberts and Cox (2003: 385). However, for the reasons outlined in this chapter and throughout this book, these are not the right research contexts for discussing the Pagan or other British repatriation debates. In the British Isles there is a dual situation: our museums and some teaching institutions hold anthropological remains from the New World, many of which were collected from named individuals within living memory for scientific study. It is these that most closely fit the New World debate and form part of our post-colonial legacy. However, there is also a second type of remains; those of people who died in this country as part of either British prehistory or history. These individuals and the collections of their remains are not helpfully placed in the New World context. They are part of a European past and should be displayed, researched and interacted with as a form of commemoration, to remember who they were and share the human experience across all of its contexts, both ancient and modern.

The display of the dead has been debated from both a New World and a Pagan perspective. Many museums within the UK and further afield store and display human remains, and as a result there is some discussion about their ethical position. Body Worlds, an international exhibition, has engendered a debate in the UK and USA about the need for permission to display the recently dead (Barilan 2006), in this case granted before they die through permission and donation forms. However, a similar debate has spread to surround ancient human remains: is it ethical to display our ancestors, even if they cannot now provide their own permissions? Certainly the idea of permission is a modern cultural position derived from an Anglo-American preoccupation with 'hyper-individualism'. For example, the challenges to Body Worlds have varied in different countries: in Munich, Germany, the legal challenge focused on the remains having not been buried, as is lawfully required of dead bodies and cremations; in France a copy-cat show was shut down over issues of respect, and it was argued that the proper place for a body was in a cemetery (Chrisafis 2009); and in Israel the challenge has focused on dignity and religious sensitivities (Zarchin & Eyadat 2009).

In January 2006 the World Archaeology Congress adopted the Tamaki Makau-rau Accord which outlines a code of ethics for the display of the dead. The Accord indicates that this permission should be sought from affected groups. However, it is most applicable to indigenous communities of the New World where individual affected groups are easily identified. In Old World countries it is difficult to ascertain who the affected groups are and so the opinion of the general public has often been felt to provide authority. But the museum-going public seems to be largely behind the archaeological and scientific display of the dead. It is after all one of the places where they can interact with the past as well as witness dead bodies, and through that interaction experience their own humanity. This does not mean that the display of the dead is uncontested, and such a debate takes place as museums struggle to find their role in modern society and the funds they need to survive.

The display of human remains

Body Worlds
One of the purposes of museums is to display cultural artefacts for entertainment and education. However, this display is affected by the fact that museums are increasingly short of funds and increasingly artistic in their layout, which raises questions about the manner of display of human remains. The Historic Scotland policy is not to display human remains of any type or of any age in any of its properties (Historic Scotland 2006). In England, however, the display of human tissue has extended into other venues and in 2009 the O2 display space in London's Millennium Dome hosted a return of the Body Worlds exhibition, a historically contentious display of recently deceased bodies preserved through the technique of plastination (see e.g. Brooks & Rumsey 2007). However, with two recent back-to-back exhibitions in the UK, can the display of human remains in this way be truly described as contentious?

The most obvious question, and one on which the display of modern bodies in the USA and the UK has hinged, is one of consent. Despite ongoing controversy surrounding Body Worlds, which suggested that some individuals used in the exhibition had not given consent to plastination, a commission by the California Science Centre (2004) in the USA was able to match death certificates and body donation forms and so verified informed legal consent of the bodies. This was repeated in the UK at the request of the Human Tissue Authority which regulated and licensed both of the recent exhibitions. The same has not always been found to be true of Body Worlds' direct competitors.

Body Worlds is a popular exhibition, and between 1996 and 2009 twenty-nine million people from three continents including Asia, Europe and North America visited it (Institute for Plastination 2009). Indeed, the return of Body Worlds to Britain twice after the controversial media coverage of the 2002 London exhibition highlights an extremely important point: the public reaction and media reaction to the exhibition have been very different.

Walter (2004a, 2004b) has put the press coverage in perspective. He argues that the attitude of the British media had been established by events like the scandals of Alder Hey and Anthony-Noel Kelly (see Chapter 2). He states that:

When Body Worlds came to London in 2002, it therefore found itself in a society where the dead and human remains are rarely on view, yet where the alleged misuse of dead bodies by artists and doctors was an ongoing scandal. (Walter 2004a: 611-12)

Indeed, art critics for the *Guardian* did not accuse the 2002 exhibition of a lack of dignity or of being disrespectful to the dead body but indicated that: 'It has little to do with art, even though the anatomist's work is hugely artful' (Searle 2002). Moreover, Professor Gunther von Hagens, the scientific inventor of modern plastination, and the exhibition designer, was likened to the artist Joseph Beuys (Jeffries 2002) or stage director Jonathan Miller (Searle 2002) and perhaps also predictably to Frankenstein (Jackson 2002).

The *Guardian* (Harris & Connolly 2002) also linked the exhibition to the international trade in illicit cadavers and more explicitly to the Alder Hey scandal (Chrisafis 2002). Other journalists (Jackson 2002) were more direct but still emotive and questioned the educational remit of the exhibition. Certainly some of this reaction stems from the fact that the British show was first held in the Atlantis Gallery, an art gallery, rather than a museum or scientific display space. In similar shows, as early as 1998, Manhattan exhibition art

4. Display, repatriation and respect for the dead

critics were questioning whether the display was art or merely 'post-modern entertainment in the worst possible taste' (Karacs 1998). However, the use of art galleries at this early stage of the global Body Worlds phenomenon happened because these institutions are often private spaces and so more willing to host the show than government-funded museums, not because its creators regarded what they did as art.

Von Hagens continues to use artistically and classically posed bodies, thus positioning his work into an artistic tradition and heritage; however, he also depicts bodies in motion performing sports, for example: fencing, basketball and chess (see Fig. 7), and in poses designed to expose and allow compari-

Fig. 7. A plastinated man playing chess. Reproduced with kind permission, © Gunther von Hagens' Body Worlds and the Institute for Plastination, www.bodyworlds.com.

son of particular parts of the human anatomy, for example: the womb, muscles and brain. Thus while some of what he does can be described as artistic, it could be better considered as science, education or an invitation to view human anatomy – an invitation that, before this 2002 exhibition, had only been open to those anatomists, researchers and medics allowed into Britain's anatomy museums (Walter 2004a).

Body Worlds has arguably become more successful than the touring exhibition Treasures of Tutankhamen, one of the most successful museum exhibitions ever, and has certainly been accepted by the public as an educational and valuable experience. A national counter-campaign by the Bishop of Manchester to Body Worlds 4 was able to attract only 41 signatures to his government e-petition (Marshall 2009).

Unlike most archaeological remains, bodies which have undergone plastination can stand upright and so inhabit the same space as the viewer. As a result Body Worlds is able to forgo the glass cases of more traditional museums which separate the public from the display. New exhibition designs for museums, like the Terracotta Army exhibition in London in 2009, where the figures stood upright and were not behind glass, arguably have a similar effect.

Skeletons: London's Buried Bones
Despite having rather more traditionally displayed human remains laying flat in display cases, Skeletons: London's Buried Bones, organised and hosted by the Wellcome Trust between 23 July and 28 September 2008, was described as: 'a show that probes the most intimate recesses of human existence' by the *The Times* (Vine 2008). Unlike the first incarnation of Body Worlds, the show was not dressed up to be artistic, and the biographies of the human remains were highlighted rather than hidden. It displayed 26 examples from the *c.*17,000 skeletons stored by the Museum of London to tell selected stories that led the exhibition visitor through an account of London's past, using London's dead, from the Roman period to the nineteenth century. The show encompassed the results of scientific

Fig. 8. Visitors experiencing the 'Skeletons' exhibition. Reproduced with kind permission of Wellcome Images.

investigations and photographs of where the skeletons were found projected onto a screen pinpointing the location of these sites, to tell human stories about London's dead (see Fig. 8). Geographic references enabled visitors to appreciate the history visually, and so, at least experientially, the ancient dead occupied London present.

The feedback from visitors was very positive. Given that the advertising for the exhibition was a close-up of a skull, artistically lit and set against a black background, it is likely that people who did not want to see human skeletons did not choose to visit the exhibition. Just two visitors commented: 'While fascinating, I am uncertain as to whether human remains should be put on public display' and 'Does no one stop to think and contemplate what right do we have to put human remains on display?' (Aldous & Payne 2009: 35). However, the majority of people were very interested in seeing the effects of disease on the skeletons and in contemplating their own life: 'All good. Doubt these people would have moaned about the NHS' and

'Thought-provoking and beautifully presented. Makes me wonder about how self absorbed we are about our health despite our affluence, when these humans survived so much and healed' (Aldous & Payne 2009: 35).

In a report on the public reactions Aldous & Payne (2009: 34) indicated that 754 people (94%) of the customer feedback was positive and just 9 people (1%) left negative comments describing the display as boring or disappointing. This contrasts with 12 describing it as 'beautiful', 18 as 'wonderful', 27 as 'amazing' and 'fantastic', and at the top end of the scale 178 people described the show as 'interesting' and 118 as 'fascinating' or 'very interesting ... and treated with a great deal of respect'. It is unlikely that plastic reconstructions of the skeletons could have elicited such an emotive response, even from self-selecting groups of visitors, some of whom chose to leave comments. This exhibition inspired people to think beyond their own experience by appreciating the experiences of others first hand, for example their struggles with pain and illness, which is 'something a textbook just cannot give you' (Aldous & Payne 2009: 35).

Lindow Man, Manchester
Just two comments from the feedback about the Skeletons exhibition asked questions about the right of modern cultures to display the bodies of the dead. However, Manchester Museum took a temporary exhibition of the Lindow Man bog body as an opportunity to ask a similar question, specifically: 'what Lindow Man means to us today.' In this exhibition seven people from different contexts provided their own perspectives on the Lindow Man bog body, his life and death. The opinions of these people had been reached through a successful and in many ways progressive consultation process. The exhibition has attracted criticism for the position of the remains, which are come upon as if by accident within the designed display space, and for the unfinished appearance of the exhibition, particularly the plywood boards holding the text (see Fig. 9). It has been suggested that it comes over as a self-indulgent exercise and not one which actually presented Lindow Man, who he was

Fig. 9. Manchester Museum's Lindow Man exhibition and display boards. Reproduced with kind permission of Manchester Museum.

and what archaeologists know about him, his life and times or other bog bodies from Britain and Europe (Bienkowski 2009). Rather it aimed to consider what we as people and a society think about him, a stance that was not always well received from within the scientific or museum community, for example:

> My next impression from a first reading of the text on some of the walls was that the information and conclusions of each of the 7 persons were presented as of equal value: a Druid's on a par with the Professor who had been brought in to supervise the investigation, with those of the men who had found the body etc. And that the exhibition itself was, as I had inferred from the website, focused on Lindow Man: I found no reference to finds of other humans buried in peat/bogs. My confusion became anger: leaving aside subjectivity and knowledge and the off-handed presentation of Lindow Man himself, the exhibitors seemed unaware of the possibility of degrees of

103

detached knowledge (and therefore utility) ... . I left dissatisfied, very dissatisfied (comments left by Mr Charlton, Manchester Museum 2009).

... this exhibition is almost entirely devoid of information or balance. This is the danger of this vox pop approach to galleries. ... It even fails in that most important of pursuits in modern museums: it's boring for families. (Schofield 2008)

And criticism from contributors to the exhibition:

The rough dark boards add to the sense of the whole exhibition being half completed, or even half conceived. It would be easy to feel that it gave a profound impression of a lack of respect. (Restall Orr 2008)

Regardless of these individual feelings, the exhibition attracted 133,413 visitors during the year in which it was open (Manchester Museum 2009) and won the temporary exhibition design category of the Design Week Awards in December 2009. In the museum's own analysis of its feedback on the display it has indicated that there were two general types of comments left by visitors – those commenting on the exhibition and those answering the question: 'Should museums display human remains?' Between July and September 2008, 375 answered the question and 91% were in favour of display, and 77% had 'broadly positive comments about the exhibition'. They also claimed that, in the second quarter analysed between October and December 2008, the comments left a similar pattern, where 92% of comments about human remains were pro display in the museum, and where 90% of visitors had a 'broadly positive view of the exhibition'. Bienkowski (2009) goes on to discuss the reaction, indicating that the negative feedback – the minority of responses received – was from people who described themselves as 'expert' or experienced museum visitors. Much of the anger expressed in this feedback, some disproportionate to the exhibition itself, was directed at the exhibition about Lindow Man, not at Lindow Man himself, indeed: 'museums find themselves in an interesting position. They find themselves criticised by community groups for not integrating their perspectives sufficiently, and criticised by established audiences who no longer see their own values reflected' (Bienkowski 2009).

A display of human remains in this format seems to leave some questions that need answering. In this example the exhibition, and its establishment evaluation, do not seem to have been directed at Lindow Man, so was it necessary to use his body in such an overtly political way? Museum funding is constantly being cut or questioned; the place of museums in society is being reinterpreted, as is the role of individual curators within them. So it is natural for there to be questions about these institutions' roles and their future. However, Lindow Man is a locally contentious issue and this exhibition was sold as 'Lindow Man comes home to his roots' (Kirby 2007) in the local press. Many people argue he should be permanently displayed in Cheshire, not London, and the Lindow Primary School choir even recorded a song: 'Lindow Man we want you back again.' So, among this quite strong local and national feeling, is it right for a museum to use contested remains for its own ambitions?

Certainly the Lindow Man exhibition was contentious and has raised a debate. It also attracted national interest, and so Manchester Museum achieved some of its ambitions. It also went about the process in a very open and inclusive fashion using a process of consultation which included community groups, interest groups and establishment representatives to arrive at the form of display. But as the individually cited comments suggest (Mr Charlton was a museum professional, Schofeld a reporter, and Restel Orr a representative of a special interest group), by attempting to please everyone the Lindow Man exhibition failed to please those groups with a vested interest in the display, although it did prove popular with the general public.

This exhibition has raised some important questions and it has contributed positively to the debate about the role of museums in the display of human remains, asking questions which were also relevant to the Ancient Egyptian mummies on display upstairs. Importantly, both of these exhibitions highlight the question: would Manchester have removed the mummies after the Lindow Man exhibition if the general public's reaction had been 'No we should not display human remains?' However it seems unlikely that the museum would have received a negative response about the display of the mummies from a group of people who chose to visit the display of human remains.

I selected three different case studies to represent here. There are plenty of other permanent displays of human remains, but my selection displays different contexts. Body Worlds is now an international concern with its headquarters in Heidelberg, Germany, and it arranges its own European exhibitions in open spaces, as these avoid the bureaucratic publicly-funded museums which are very slow in the organisational process. For example, the planning procedure for Lindow Man started in or around 2005. In the USA Body Worlds' partner deals with science museums (Walter, personal communication). Similarly Skeletons was a one-off event hosted by the Wellcome Trust which has a particular interest in biomedical and medical humanities and in the public engagement with these sciences. By contrast, Lindow Man was in the Manchester Museum which is the only 'traditional' museum in this selection. Consequently it is the only organisation I have included that is both directly and indirectly funded by the government (funders include Manchester University; the Arts and Humanities Research Council; the Museums, Libraries and Archives Council (Manchester Museum 2007)) and has to compete with other similar institutions to attract funds and the museum-going public. The context of these exhibitions is very important; it determines the level of investment, the freedom of the exhibition designers and the levels of collaboration required to put on a single event and, as can be seen in these three examples, it also determines the nature of the exhibition itself.

Viewing the dead, tradition or taboo in modern society?
From each of these cases I have described here it is clear that the majority of the public who participated were happy to see human remains in museums, and many people will have travelled to see them. A small survey with 220 responses, carried out by Cambridge Archaeology, revealed that 79% of people asked expect to see human skeletons on display in museums, and 73% regard that as appropriate (Carroll 2005). A similar survey of 300 visitors to the British Museum's Egyptian collections revealed that 83% thought that mummies should be displayed, 78% thought that there was no need for more respect to be shown to the remains and 99% of respondents felt there was no need to return those remains to Egypt (Kilmister 2003: 61-2). In this second case, as with the questions raised at Manchester, it is unlikely that the response would have been negative as the audience was self-selecting and had chosen to visit a collection of mummies, indeed HAD conducted a similar survey in Suffolk in 2007 and obtained 74 responses from members of a local Pagan group and visitors to the West Stow visitors centre (HAD 2007). These results showed that 60% of respondents thought 'pre-Christian burial sites should be treated as places of sanctity', *c.* 52% believed 'Human remains should always be reburied after archaeological analysis' and *c.* 50% disagreed that the 'Display of human remains in museums is acceptable'. In all three of these surveys the number of responses was low, and the questions themselves or the context within which they were asked may have elicited particular responses. More recently a professional survey was commissioned by English Heritage in which 1,004 individuals were surveyed by phone: 91% agreed that museums should be able to display human remains and store them for research purposes, though many also agreed that they should be at least 100 years old (Mills & Tranter 2010).

There is a popular myth that the dead are hidden in modern society (after Ariès 1981), and that they are taboo (Sayer 2010), but all of these surveys, exhibitions and the ongoing discussion between scholars, interest groups and the public would seem to suggest that this is not the case. In fact modern sociological literature suggests that it is the medicalisation of dying in modern society which has caused death to be hidden or turned into a technical specialty (e.g. Walter 1994). This is reflected, and possibly countered, by the growth of new medical sub-disciplines which attempt to humanise hospital and hospice dying; certainly Alder Hey comprised a medical scandal of clandestine behaviour involving the collecting of human remains without consent, and not one about the display of the dead.

Tony Walter regards plastination, and possibly public display, as simply a modern alternative to more traditional types of disposal of the dead (Walter 2004a), much as mummification was in ancient and not so ancient societies. He argues that the visibility, or invisibility, of the dead has much less to do with global modernity, or the denial of death, than it does to do with national and local culture, institutions, traditions, histories and religion in a particular region (Walter 2005; forthcoming). Walter outlines 17 ways in which the dead can be viewed in modern societies for 'mourning, education, religious ritual, tourism, and entertainment'. England has somewhat fewer mechanisms than other countries, for there is no tradition of wakes or open coffins, nor do the English exhume their dead publicly for reburial. However, with the policy of not displaying human remains established by Heritage Scotland, and with museums choosing similar policies, the Scots may have even fewer opportunities than do the English and the Welsh to see the dead. Interestingly, this situation may have been caused indirectly by the over-medicalisation of death in England, and not through a cultural distaste for the presentation of the dead in museums.

The contrast between the policies of English and Scottish heritage organisations is a good indicator of the current state of museums within British society. They are trying to find a role within modernity and with an uncertain future they have positioned themselves, and human remains, with spirituality (see e.g. Curtis 2004), banned their display (in Scotland) or publicly questioned their own traditions (Manchester Museum). Despite this, new ways of viewing the dead emerge through medical exhibitions, the opening up of English anatomy museums to the public, or the creation of new technologies of display such as Body Worlds. In this context, where the public express support though visiting displays, and where such exhibitions provide them with a rare and important opportunity to experience death and the dead, then an appropriate question is not necessarily *whether* it is right to display human remains, but *how* they should be displayed.

The role of the museum is changing, as Jenkins (2008: 114) puts it, 'from keepers to sharers', and with this other responsibilities that have traditionally fallen under the remit of museums have also been brought into question. The storage of human remains has been an area of global concern and human tissue has been internationally repatriated as part of an increasing awareness of the post-colonial responsibility of national institutions. The repatriation debate has been seen as beginning in North America and Australia, and has focused on questions about the authority and legitimacy of museum practice.

The repatriation and reburial of human remains

Repatriation in the New World

In North America (see Klesert and Powell 1993; Klesert and Andrews 1988; Green 1984; ACHP 1985; Hubert 1989, Zimmerman 1989) and Australia (Webb 1987) the repatriation debate has focused on the beliefs and rites of the living descendants of the dead. It has resulted in the wholesale repatriation of human remains to indigenous groups – a situation that still causes alarm among North American archaeologists, whose research was, and in some circumstances still is, threatened. Since the 1960s indigenous people have waged campaigns to redress the theft of cultural property, including their ancestors, and for the prevention of the destruction of ancient and more recent burial grounds. In 1995 a BBC programme, Bones of Contention, highlighted a cultural discrepancy, or indeed racism, from the mid-twentieth century. One example used during the programme was of a cemetery exhumation in Iowa in 1971 (the result of a road building scheme over a prisoners' cemetery) and saw the exhumation of nineteenth-century indigenous remains as well as Caucasian North Americans. The indigenous remains were shipped off to a museum collection, in stark contrast to the remains of the Caucasians which were re-interred in a Christian cemetery. This set of circumstances is not an isolated example:

> Similar events occurred at the site of Custer's last stand at the Little Bighorn where the remains of the US Army soldiers found during archaeological excavation were reburied, while those of the Lakota warriors were not. (Parker Pearson 1999: 173)

Unsurprisingly these, and other situations like them, sparked off a conflict over Native American remains. They also facilitated the further discovery by Native Americans of 'surprising' numbers of indigenous remains within US institutions, and led to widespread calls for their repatriation from within indigenous groups across North America and Canada (Zimmerman 1987). This is very similar to the situation which unfolded in Australia (Webb 1987). Native Americans and the Aboriginal people from Australia had been the victims of cultural and institutional racism, their lands had been taken and now their ancestors had been desecrated and treated disrespectfully. It is perhaps unsurprising that the subsequent conflicts became so politicised. Here was an opportunity to make a stand and fight for the rights of politically marginalised living communities.

In 1989 the World Archaeology Congress council, held in South Dakota, drew up the Vermillion Accord on Human Remains. This was subsequently adopted by the World Archaeology Congress in 1990 (Roberts 2009: 19). In 1976 the state of Iowa passed reburial legislation to provide state funds to recover human remains, and a state cemetery where ancient remains could be re-interred was established. The national debate followed a similar line: in 1989 the National Museum of the American Indian Act and in 1990 the Native American Graves Protection and Repatriation Act (NAGPRA) were passed, obliging institutions to inventory and publish their collections within a given time frame, then to have that information circulated to potentially interested tribes, and finally to respond to requests from potentially affiliated groups for possible repatriation. In many cases this has not resulted in the wholesale destruction of archaeological collections as was first feared; rather, the unprecedented mobilisation of scientific resources needed to identify the appropriate groups that these skeletons belonged to has resulted in unforeseen opportunities to study bones that would otherwise have been forgotten (Smith 2004). More recently the World Archaeology Congress adopted the Tamaki Makau-rau Accord on the Display of Human Remains and Sacred Objects, a manifesto which outlines the ethical display of ancient bodies to the public (Roberts 2009: 19).

One case particularly highlights the nature of the ongoing debates surrounding human remains in North America. The case of Kennewick Man is now well known in the UK and further afield, as it has been widely discussed since the body was discovered in 1996 under the surface of Lake Wallula, Kennewick, Washington (see Chatters 2002; Fine-Dare 2002; Hurst 2000; Jones 2005; McManamon 2004; Parker Pearson 1999). Because of NAGPRA, the US Army Corps of Engineers, on whose land the discovery was made, confiscated the body from archaeologists with the intention of allowing it to be reburied on the Umatilla Indian Reservation (McManamon 2004). Five Native American groups have subsequently claimed these remains. This seizure was challenged in the Federal Courts, who decided that the Army had not acted impartially, and despite the Vermillion Accord and NAGPRA Kennewick Man was studied to determine his ethnicity and archaeological importance. Indeed, because Kennewick Man was of such age no kinship link could be established with any modern descent group and the Acts could not apply (Owsley and Jantz 2002). Calibrated radiocarbon dates suggest with a 95% probability a date between cal BP 9510-9405 and cal BP 9345-9320 (around 7500-7300 years old) making the remains one of the oldest bodies from North America. Some commentators have described the controversy as a 'superheated rhetoric' pitting the desires of scientists against Native Americans, a situation which McManamon describes as ignoring:

> ... the detailed, intensive, and wide-ranging scientific investigation of the Kennewick remains undertaken to determine the facts relevant to the questions in the case and report them (McManamon 2004).

Although the Court of Appeal found that a cultural link between the tribes and the skeleton was not proved, their claims for reburial are still, in the eyes of the indigenous community, unanswered, as for them to deny that they are the descendants of Kennewick Man is for the State to deny their religious beliefs, which describe their origin in that territory (see Jones 2005; Fine-Dare 2002).

In America the introduction of legislation to protect Native American interests has not removed the opportunity to do research. The remains of internationally significant finds have also been studied within this framework and most recently the requirements for repatriation have relied on demonstrated kinship or biological lineage. This does not mean that the US authorities have relaxed their legal protection of Native American cultural resources. In June 2009 'the biggest bust ever of thieves who take ancient Native American artefacts from public lands' (Riccardi 2009) took place. Many of the stolen artefacts that were recovered, which were valued at over $335,000, came from burial sites, sending a clear message of intolerance towards grave-robbing (Riccardi & Tankersley 2009). Unfortunately, a day after his arrest for allegedly selling a tribal bird pendant, Dr James Redd, a 60-year-old medical doctor from Utah, killed himself. A few days later Steven Shrader, 56, another suspect in this case, also killed himself following his arrest (Yardley 2009). Despite these unfortunate incidents, things have at least partially come full circle: in this example the Federal government enthusiastically protected the resources that the Native Americans had had to fight for just a few decades previously. The repatriation of human remains from government institutions is a process that 'helps Native American groups to achieve some closure on traumatic events of their history' (Thornton 2002: 22).

Britain and post-colonial repatriation

In 2007 the Science Museum returned the remains of Tasmanian aborigines to their ethnic home (Henderson 2007). This event highlights the post-colonial reality of storing foreign human remains in British museum collections. It demonstrates that Britain is not separate from these post-colonial issues. In Tasmania and mainland Australia the question of aboriginal repatriation is linked with the question of their identity and their 'ancestors' (Fforde 2002), and in Britain these arguments about ancestors have been successful in securing repatriation.

Interestingly, Britain has been involved in the repatriation of colonially obtained remains since 1947, when the Governor of Ceylon wrote on behalf of the Vidyalankhara Student Association to the conservator of the anthropology collection at the Museum of the Phrenological Society, Edinburgh. The purpose of the letter was to ask if they held the skull of Keppitipola Nilama, which was removed without authorisation in the mid-nineteenth century. The conservator replied that they did indeed have the skull. Given that there was probably a political motivation behind the request, the museum was happy to concede to the wishes of the Governor and the skull was returned later that year (Fforde 2004: 119-20). The Ceylon repatriation case is the earliest Fforde discovered and she suggests that, at least in these early cases, the scientific value of remains under question was not a serious consideration.

Fforde (2004) describes repatriation events within the UK during the 1980s and 1990s, before the passing of the 2004 Human Tissue Act (see Chapter 2), which made it possible for

113

museums to de-accession human remains 'reasonably believed to be of a person who died less that 1,000 years before this section comes into force' i.e. AD 1004 (Human Tissue Act section 47: 2). In contrast to the 1947 repatriation, Fforde describes a much less successful situation for repatriation campaigners with a number of protests held outside large British museums. However, in 1989 St Thomas's Hospital transferred three aboriginal skulls, one articulated post-cranial skeleton, and a wooden club to the Australian High Commission without being asked for them. In 1990 Tasmanian Aboriginals approached the Royal College of Surgeons, Dublin, who later returned a named individual who had died in 1830. Also in 1990 remains were repatriated from Glasgow Art Gallery, Peterborough City Museum, Bradford University and the Pitt Rivers Museum, Oxford. However, these were all small collections, and the University of Edinburgh was the only UK institution with large collections that conceded to these requests after a university-wide debate in which it was agreed that repatriation was appropriate. The actual act of repatriation was slow, because of the lack of funds from Australia; however, the second part was completed in 2000, including the return of at least one named individual – Tommy Walker (Fforde 2004: 119-26).

Since the passing of the Human Tissue Act several high profile cases have been reported in the newspapers and caused national debate. One of the first was reported in 2006 when Baroness Helena Kennedy QC, a trustee of the British Museum (Kennedy 2006), reported on the decision by the British Museum to repatriate two kangaroo skin bundles of cremated human ash to Tasmania. Despite the fact that these are 'now the only two such bundles known anywhere in the world' (Kennedy 2006) the trustees decided to repatriate the objects based on what would be most beneficial to the public.

In 2006 the Science Museum approached Australian Aboriginals with the intention of repatriating remains from their collection to Tasmania. The Science Museum held 19,500 specimens, of which just over 10,000 were from the British Isles, 450 from Australia and 24 from Tasmania (Henderson

4. Display, repatriation and respect for the dead

2006). The majority of these remains were collected in the early nineteenth century by George Augustus Robinson (Henderson 2006) and by the mid-nineteenth century, as a consequence of British colonisation, only 15 Tasmanians were still alive (Henderson 2007). This makes the remains in the Science Museum extremely important for historical and scientific research, but also for surviving Aboriginal groups. After the museum agreed a schedule of repatriation it started a three-month long research programme to recover as much information as possible before the 24 specimens were returned to Tasmania. However, it was stopped when the Tasmanian Aboriginal Centre took out an injunction in February 2007 to prevent intrusive research such as DNA analysis. The remains were flown to Tasmania on 11 May 2007; it was agreed that they would be held by the Tasmanian Aboriginal Centre and that both parties would have to agree to their destruction, either by cremation by the Tasmanians, or as a consequence of DNA extraction for scientific investigation (Henderson 2007).

The post-colonial situation means there is arguably a global responsibility to help rebuild the identities and cultures of people around the world, and the repatriation of human remains seems to have become a recognised means to facilitate the reconstruction of indigenous identities. Certainly it is within this context of 'post-colonial guilt' that Fforde (2004) positioned her argument. She described a culture of theft, collection and curiosity by early anthropologists within a colonial world view which drove the collection of the remains currently held in British institutions. Most of these remains, particularly those in small collections which have not been studied, have limited contextual information and are not just anthropological specimens but the physical remains of the development of racist arguments. They have been part of the justification for ethnic discriminations which marred the nineteenth and early twentieth centuries.

There is, however, another context within which repatriation should be considered: the changing role of the museum in British society. Sociologist Tiffany Jenkins (2008) approaches the problem from a different perspective and regards museums as having to find a new place in the world where the industry has been 'reinventing itself as an authoritative voice of thera-peutic recognition' (Jenkins 2008: 115). Certainly, after the Second World War, restitution and reparations for past wrongs became a major part of German culture, just as the perceived wrongs of the atomic bomb at Hiroshima are commemorated across the world, for example the Peace Gardens in Sheffield which were dedicated to the memory of Hiroshima.

Jenkins saw the museum's new role of restitution and com-munity participation as a result of the erosion of its original (nineteenth-century) role of authoritative education in the name of science and scholarship (Jenkins 2008: 114). Museums hold many objects and although human remains are arguably not simply objects, it is notable that to avoid the loss of collections for financial or political reasons it is illegal for some institutions to de-accession any museum objects without permission (British Museum Act 1963, National Heritage Act 1983). This changed with the Human Tissue Act of 2004. However, one survey re-vealed that claims from overseas indigenous groups to English institutions totalled just 33 with some of these being repeat claims, and in seven cases the return of material had already been agreed (Weeks & Bott 2003: 10, 16). So what is the role of museums in this issue: healers of the disenfranchised or protec-tors of the physical remains of our past and present? If museums should be thinking in broader terms than simply 'who walks through their doors' (Kennedy 2006), then repatriation should not be seen as an easy answer. While it may serve to assuage English 'guilt' at past crimes, if it does not preserve the physical evidence of those crimes then there is a danger that they will be forgotten. By comparison, consider what would be the result if someone chose to destroy the physical evidence of holocaust?

By giving back the ancestors of the indigenous people, Tas-manian, Australian and to a lesser extent North American governments, who fund these reparations, can feel that they are absolved of the sins of the past. However, the danger is that resources are not available to fulfil the needs of the politically and socially marginalised indigenous populations that remain. There is a risk that limited political empowerment, seen in the initial successes of the repatriation movements, has been replaced by cheap and temporary fixes that do not resolve deeper social problems. In the long run repatriation may only serve to ease the guilt of the west and will not solve the problems of educational and economic marginalisation. Worldwide, the institutions which are returning human remains must ask if they are participating in valid reparations or actively engaged in further economic marginalisation and seclusion that simply extend the wrongs done in the colonial era. The question of repatriation of human remains does not get any easier with time, and each individual claim should be considered on its own merits, and within its own political, historic and global context.

Reburial outside the post-colonial context
Repatriation of the dead does not have to result from conflict but can be driven by research interest and indeed by the emotive power that individual human remains can exert. Individual cases should be considered carefully, for example the repatriation of Arthur Dillon, archbishop of Narbonne and primate of Languedoc, France. His body was discovered at King's Cross St Pancras in 2003 (Emery 2006). Shortly afterwards archaeologists approached Narbonne Cathedral directly, but initially they were not interested in the remains. Arthur Dillon was then re-interred in a sealed, labelled box close to the rest of the remains exhumed from King's Cross St Pancras. This proved to be a particularly insightful move by Phil Emery, archaeological consultant for the St Pancras project, who was later approached by Jacques Michaud, a French archaeologist, about the body. Arthur Dillon was re-exhumed and in 2007 a French newspaper reported that the Catholic congregation of Narbonne were able to celebrate his return (*L'Indépendent* 2007). Dillon was given a coffin draped in the Languedoc coat of arms and conveyed in a wooden ceremonial hearse accompanied by city officials. Two centuries after his death he had returned to a full ceremonial and Catholic funeral.

This repatriation is important: it is the successful collaboration of archaeologists from two different countries, Jacques
Michaud and Phil Emery. It was also a collaboration which
shows what informed proactive archaeologists can achieve by
considering not only the need to rebury but also the most
appropriate form that a reburial should take; Dillon was a
French archbishop from an Irish family buried in Anglican
London. Even though the Cathedral authorities did not recognise the cultural significance of this repatriation event,
archaeologists did. It was through their intervention that people at this civic ceremony could take pride, not just in local
French politics but in Anglo-French relations. After all, Dillon
was discovered during the extension to the railway platform
that would allow Eurostar to have its London terminus at St
Pancras International.

The Arthur Dillon reburial case stands in stark contrast to
that of Anne Mowbray (see Chapter 2). The two examples are
separated by 43 years and a completely different set of circumstances. Anne Mowbray's body was forcibly repatriated to allow
reburial in Westminster Abbey, whereas Arthur Dillon's body
was at first rejected, and then repatriated and reburied with a
similarly symbolic funeral. It was archaeologists who recognised the cultural significance that such an event would have.
This contrast probably does not represent a cultural shift in
archaeologists' behaviour; if Anne Mowbray had not been forcibly repatriated there is every indication that she would have
been voluntarily handed over to the appropriate individuals.
However, it does demonstrate that context is fundamental
when considering each individual case. The Jewbury reburial
shares some aspects with Anne Mowbray, in that scientific
examination was forcibly stopped and the remains confiscated
and independently reburied. However, it also stands in contrast to cases such as St Albans, when the Anglican and
Catholic authorities worked alongside archaeologists in 1978 to
respectfully exhume, examine and then re-inter the bodies of
medieval monks, including the father of the only male English
pope (see Chapter 3).

With the exception of Jewbury, these cases all focus on particular named individuals. But successful reburial also takes place outside these circumstances. St Peter's Church, Barton-upon-Humber, North Lincolnshire, saw the reburial of over 3,000 skeletons (some from the early eleventh century) in 2008 within a specially designed ossuary which cost over £600,000 to build. As a mark of respect the pastor conducted the ceremony in Old English, and an individual who was found in a wooden coffin was returned to that same coffin (BBC Look North 2009).

Similar stories are not uncommon. On 4 October 2009 the Lord's Prayer was said in Old English, Latin and Modern English when the bodies of 57 Anglo-Scandinavians (AD 679-1011) were re-interred in the grounds of St Mary's Church in Masham, North Yorkshire. They had been discovered in a nearby medieval cemetery which was being developed to build public facilities in the Little Market Place (Dooks 2009). Reburial of historic remains has also taken place informally and outside a Christian context. An independent museum, the Museum of Witchcraft, which is one of the most popular tourist destinations in Cornwall, decided to rebury a skeleton in its collection. The body, allegedly that of Joan Wytte, a notorious Cornish witch who died in Bodmin Gaol in 1813, hung in the museum in front of a coffin (Museum of Witchcraft 2009). The curator decided that the museum display was not respectful. He removed all the wire pins that held her together, and reburied her secretly in a local wood with a few simple gravegoods: a small bottle of brandy, a clay pipe and tobacco (Garner 1998). In the case of Joan Wytte the term reburial might be better substituted with burial, as she may never have been buried in the first instance.

Reburial and British Paganism
The predominantly Christian context of reburial has not gone unnoticed within alternative lifestyle and spiritual groups. Building on the terminology and success of indigenous communities in the New World, British Pagan groups have begun to

lay claim to ancient human remains within museum collections (Moshenska 2009; Sayer 2009; Randerson 2007; Smith & Mays 2007; Restall Orr & Bienkowski 2006a). These groups recognise that their case is different to that of historically oppressed indigenous communities as they have not suffered at the hands of western colonists. Nonetheless, Honouring the Ancient Dead (HAD), an advocacy group that aims to represent British Pagan views, based upon a council of Pagan thinkers, theologians and writers from the main strands of British Paganism, have nationally declared their desire to see the reburial of ancient human remains. However, HAD has actively dissociated itself from the various protest groups that work under the banner of the Council of British Druid Orders CoBDO, specifically because those groups' campaigns are based upon the call for mandatory reburial, whereas HAD prefers consultation, regarding reburial as desirable but not mandatory. A third group, Pagans for Archaeology, regularly campaigns against mandatory reburial.

In 2006 a representative of the CoBDO requested the reburial of prehistoric remains from within the Alexander Keiller Museum, Avebury. Indeed, within the wider Pagan context Restall Orr & Bienkowski (2006a) argued that the Pagan interests in ancient remains are 'legitimate' and that the Pagan world view is a valid alternative interpretation of the past; arguments that will be familiar to people who have followed the repatriation debate in North America and Australia.

However, there are some important differences between indigenous communities in the New World and modern western spiritual groups. One of these is that although Pagan beliefs have, in the past, been socially marginalised, Pagans are not an independent ethnic group with an alternative view of the past. They are part of western, and historically Christian, society, and through national interest groups they are facilitating the integration of Pagan beliefs into areas of British life, such as being able to use a Pagan oath in courts and having Pagan chaplains in hospitals, prisons and the military. Although many Pagans believe in the sanctity of nature, individual Pagan groups also have their origins in counter culture and protest and so are equally manifestations of the desire of individuals to disown a Christian state system in favour of what many perceive to be an older or more honest alternative. This impression is often based on idealistic notions of the past found in *The Golden Bough* or other romantic interpretations of ancient spirituality (Hutton 2001, 2007, 2009). Unlike the indigenous people of New World countries, modern westerners can choose to become Pagans and often select a system suitable for their own interests. Even Heathens, Druids and Wiccans, who are among the most popular groups, have many subgroups and subcategories that convey different belief systems (Gardnerian Wicca, Alexandrian Wicca, or one of the many different orders of British Druids). Out of this disorder the Pagan Federation aims to provide a single voice for Paganism, but on the question of reburial different views abound. For example, Pagans for Archaeology started on an internet social networking site and has expanded to host conferences which generally support the retention and study of human remains by archaeologists. Other active Pagans advocate co-operation with archaeologists who have similar ambitions, although this is often done without proposing a mechanism for that co-operation (see Wallis & Blain 2004).

Pagans and archaeologists do share an interest in the past and arguably a similar origin in seventeenth- and eighteenth-century romantic notions of history. Although Hutton (2001, 2009) disputes any tangible evidence for a connection between ancient religions and new spirituality he does champion Paganism as an important part of British society. However, archaeologists remain sceptical, relying not on notions of continuity and spirituality but on contextual and interpretive rationale and on the analysis of materials, peoples and landscapes. Herein lies one of the reasons for a clash of cultures – not disharmony in interpretive narrative, but access to that narrative.

As a profession, archaeology is divided in two: those who write about digging and those who dig. And although this is a figurative representation those who write about it are often middle-class graduates with many degrees that provide legitimacy. Essentially they are 'the establishment' and in sociological terms those on the outside of that establishment are 'other' – including Pagans who are largely disentangled from the state, organisations like PEBBLE (Public Bodies Liaison Committee for British Paganism) have existed to liaise with government as a minority faith group only since 2004-5. While Paganism has had its own past in personal and political protest it is now seeking a legitimacy of its own. One of the areas where it may do that successfully is in the liberal heritage sector where groups who are also marginalised, or 'other', have already achieved political empowerment though repatriation claims.

Although consultation may traditionally involve discussion, Restall Orr & Bienkowski (2006b) proposed a hypothetical system which would take the process one stage further. They suggested an integrated system which places interest groups into every aspect of the process of excavation, analysis and the reburial of human remains. With such a proposal it is possible to foresee a situation in which the discovery of a late sixth- or early seventh-century burial in the Upper Thames Valley would require a Heathen who followed neo-Germanic tradition, a Druid because the burial could be that of a Briton, and a Rector, just in case they had been Christian. This is clearly untenable, would add further expense to an already over-stretched commercially structured funding system, and further shows little respect to the poor individual being exhumed.

The request put to the Alexander Keiller Museum was at least partially successful, though not because remains were reburied. De-accessioning Neolithic, Bronze Age or Iron Age human remains, like those contested, is still a legal issue for some British museums because the lawful changes made in the Human Tissue Act 2004 only allow human remains under 1,000 years old to be disposed of (Human Tissue Act 2004: subsection 47:2). Even for those museum trusts where this does not apply there may be a legally binding constitutional document that disallows the de-accession of any part of their collections, although recent dialogues within the museum community favour relaxing these rules.

There is also a policy of retention within British museums designed to safeguard important collections for the present and for our future. Accordingly the Museums Association Code of Ethics requires individual museums to have a 'presumption in favour of the retention of items within the public domain' (Museums Association 2008: 24) as does Historic Scotland (2006). Alongside these responsibilities is the requirement to 'consult and involve communities ... and balance this with the role of museums in leading and promoting debate' (Museums Association 2008: 13). To comply with this regulation the Alexander Keiller Museum had to take the CoBDO's request to consultation; it did this in combination with the National Trust and English Heritage to facilitate a national debate.

In this context it is unlikely that the Druids' requests could have been met. However, as a result of this interest in ancient remains, and the wider need for a general advisory service, British archaeologists are rethinking the 2005 *Guidance for Best Practice for Treatment of Human Remains Excavated from Christian Burial Grounds in England,* and the corresponding advisory panel which will cover all burial in England – the Advisory Panel on the Archaeology of Burials in England – and have added the need to consult with outside interest groups during the drawing up of advisory documents for guiding the excavation process. This panel does not, however, offer advice to museums (Thackray & Payne 2008; White 2009).

Individual Pagans may be interested in the fate of archaeological collections, but there is a danger that requests for reburial, particularly mandatory reburial, serve a more political than spiritual purpose, providing a means of legitimating the position of a more extreme and unrepresentative element of British Paganism. Using the dead in this way cannot be seen as respectful of those individuals. Indeed, reburial may not even be appropriate; the West Kennet skeletons, for example, were not technically buried in the first place, they were entombed.

Moreover, the archaeological evidence suggests that they were used, reused and moved around – dead humans were witnessed by our ancestors and used as a cultural resource over several generations, even without particular identities in some cases. Their use today as unnamed cultural remains is not inconsistent with ancient post-mortem behaviour, nor is the political use of the dead: for example previous uses of the past as a form of legitimating a present (see Bradley & Williams 1998). Archaeological arguments and counterarguments can be discussed over and over, but what is undeniable is that archaeologists do not actually know what our ancestors thought about their dead or their funerary customs. As a result, reburial may not be an appropriate answer to modern problems, but one thing that archaeologists and Pagans may agree on is the need to treat them with respect, as both ancestors and irreplaceable cultural resources.

Discussion

In North America, Australia and other countries with a post-colonial past, repatriation is deeply connected with perceptions of identity, empowerment and reparations within global and historic frameworks. In Australia, the repatriation debate can be traced back to the 1960s, and by the 1980s the scientific community no longer contested Aboriginal claims on named individuals (Fforde 2002). However, the Aboriginal campaigners regarded named and unnamed individuals alike as their 'ancestors'. The world community was not so responsive, and in 1984 scientists argued that this material was often too old and of too great a scientific importance to be owned by particular groups to the detriment of the global community (Fforde 2002). Indeed, it is clear that there is a difference between the named and the unnamed just as there is a difference between the recent and the distant past. What this means is that the context must be considered in each individual repatriation case, especially where local, national or global politics may be more important than the remains themselves.

4. Display, repatriation and respect for the dead

The identity of the dead is important. Many reburial or repatriation claims in the UK focus on named historic individuals, and many archaeological exhibitions attempt to remove the ravages of time by re-identifying the ancient dead, giving graves or dry bones names or life stories, and thus providing a humanity which can be appreciated by a wider group of people. By contrast Body Worlds removes the identity of people before they go on display, stripping away skin and names, removing race, and by doing so re-humanising bodies after death and allowing viewers to relate their own experience of occupying a fleshy body to those of other people (*contra* Rees Leahy 2008; see Walter 2004b).

In the same way the ability for people to go to a museum and witness the diversity of humanity's past and present is important – skin deep we are all the same, 3,000 years old or not. Shared experience can help to broaden our own personal perspectives both about what it means to be alive, and what it means to be human. This perspective may be the realisation of modern medical intervention, as at Skeletons, or a connected love of marshland linking Lindow Man to the modern day residents of the North-West. It may be a perception of shared spiritual connection or the importance of landscape and personal beliefs, but one thing is universal: we could not experience the physical reality of our dead ancestors, just as our own immediate ancestors and those before them did, without some sort of control and choice. The dead are powerful and their use, or misuse, as political tools is a matter of historical record, but we should also show them respect for what they have done and what they continue to do for us today.

Respect itself is a difficult concept as it means different things to different people. If concepts of respect are irreconcilable there is a case that each individual interest group makes its own definitions and codes of conduct that describe its interactions with the ancient dead, without judging or undermining other groups' perspectives. However, where we all come together is in the display space. Manchester Museum recently covered up part of its mummy collection, also after consultation. These individuals had been unwrapped, and with it their nakedness was exposed. Complete bodies with dry skin evoke more reaction than bones in the viewer: these are more complete people, and less like the bones of more recent cemetery exhumations. The museum claims this decision was made at the request of visitors (Kennedy 2008), but even if it was not, it returns humanity to what may otherwise have been regarded as just material culture.

If archaeologists or Egyptologists are going to use the argument that elaborate ancient funerals were acts of display and immortalisation, to justify the display of people who cannot give consent today, then they should also allow them the humanity that those funeral displays contained: their objects, grave-goods and wrappings (where they remain). With modern medical scanning techniques, destructive un-wrappings or 'post-mortems' are unnecessary, dehumanising and destructive. The same applies to bones that can be *interred* within a modern display space and positioned as they were found alongside the objects with which they were originally buried. This type of display can only deepen the relationship between viewer and bodies; essentially the observer is sharing the moment of burial and what remains of that person (Sayer 2010). Like the Body Works exhibition, ancient remains can occupy emotional space with the living. Archaeology can be commemoration, not of the individual dead whose identities and personality have been forgotten but of the collective dead, the people of the past and their humanity, their struggles and their achievements, and it is this story that should be shared alongside the science of investigative practice. Viewing the dead is, on balance, both a very ancient and very modern funerary tradition.

Conclusion
The problem of modernity
and the ancient dead

In this book I have discussed a number of case studies from Britain and North America and described situations in South Africa and Australia. The idea was to address a problem which I found in the UK: that there is a tendency for examples of ethical problems to be inaccessible, and as a result the debate has focused on just a small handful of case studies to illustrate moral questions; Jewbury is the most obvious example (for a recent revisit see Payne 2009). This is in contrast to the extensively grasped and widely discussed global repatriation policies initiated by indigenous communities and diaspora populations. Studies of these are well understood in Britain, North America and Australia, and yet the requirements of communities and national politics in European countries are very different to those in North America and Australia: the debate needs to be global or there is a danger that the language and attitude of the New World will be applied inappropriately. There is already a problem as the British burial laws and the 2004 Human Tissue Act were designed to prevent the misuse of the recently dead but have ended up also providing the legal framework for archaeology.

In Chapter 1 I discussed why cemetery projects take place, outlining the relationship between continuous urban development and economic growth, and the survival of cities or towns. Sheffield was used as an example to demonstrate that there is not a single cemetery site in the town centre which is unaffected by modern development, and the most high profile and

127

visible graves are the most threatened, since they are also those most centrally located. However, this pressure to develop can be seen in different forms: the need for modern infrastructure including roads, railways, trams and civic gardens; and private development in the form of pubs and shopping centres alongside the growth or transformation of religious buildings. If the dead have meaning for modern society then these areas need serious consideration, and the nineteenth-century burial laws do not provide a suitable framework. For example, is it right to disturb the dead to dig a beer cellar in a cemetery whose occupants abstained from alcohol as part of a social observance within a religious context, especially if it is avoidable? However, it is often simply impossible to avoid cemetery development: space in towns is often more valuable or more important for use by the living than by the dead. Exhumation projects are ongoing and need to be addressed as more than just open spaces and brown field sites within the legal and planning system.

In Chapter 2 these ideas develop further through a discussion, not of why archaeologists dig the dead, but under what authority they can dig the dead. I specifically investigated the relationship between the law, lawmakers and archaeologists and used the case study of Anne Mowbray to highlight how the recent legal reinterpretation of the burial law has caused so many problems for commercial archaeologists. Archaeology in the UK has its recent origins in protest and campaign, which proved valuable in establishing modern mitigation archaeology, but this is also a historic circumstance and may explain the difficulties that some archaeologists have interacting with the media. By understanding the circumstances around the Alder Hey and Anthony-Noel Kelly scandals it is possible to see how wider social circumstances and attitudes directly and indirectly affect the archaeology of human remains. For example, who owns the dead and their belongings, if it is possible to own the dead at all? Human remains stir up emotions and the nature of personal and institutional problems affect daily practice on a legal level.

Conclusion

Chapter 3 focused on actual exhumation, but rather than the process of digging I investigated the relationship between archaeological exhumation and local or national interest groups. Within this theme a number of cases from the UK and the USA (Manhattan's African Burial Ground, Rapparee Cove, Bonn Square, Fromelles and Jewbury) demonstrate where protests caused difficulties or stopped work entirely. In many of the cases the language is couched in terms of respect, dignity and human decency, yet such emotive or subjective discussion simply shrouds the political nature of the protests. However, this can be avoided, as the protest stance is almost always triggered by a failure in communication resulting in the marginalisation of interest groups. Protest is not all bad, and building on a history of protest I looked at how archaeologists have used their special relationship with human remains to take charge of cemetery projects and safeguard sites of national and international importance from within the heritage community.

Chapter 4 investigated the role of museums as guardians of human remains in modern society and discussed two main concepts, repatriation or reburial and display. It explored repatriation from two different contexts, post-colonial global relations, using the classic Kennewick Man case study, and looking at repatriation cases from British institutions to those in Australia. It also considered the museum context from another perspective: the changing role and uncertain future of museums in modern society. From this perspective I discussed the display of dead bodies in museums using three recent exhibitions as examples: Body Worlds, the Skeletons exhibit at the Wellcome Collection and the display of Lindow Man by Manchester Museum. These examples were used to facilitate discussion, as they are not all archaeological and were certainly not all put on by archaeologists. My aim was to demonstrate that archaeologists are not the only people who deal with the dead, ancient or modern, and so within the relationship between archaeology and the public there are plenty of opportunities to see how archaeology fits into a wider social reality: the relationship between modern society and the dead.

Who owns the stories about the dead?

One of the inherent problems of modernity is the regular exclusion of parts of social life as separate from institutional life: the
dying, the old, the ill and the criminal are removed (Giddens
1991). And so are the dead. This has resulted in compartmen-
talised lives, both personal lives and social lives. Further to
this, Alder Hey provides a well learned lesson for those who
deal with the dead. The dead are inert but can act as a catalyst
for underlying social problems. However, the Alder Hey scandal is not, on closer observation, so different from Bonn Square,
or Fromelles, or any of the slave cemeteries discussed in this
book. It is simply a matter of scale. Alder Hey is a hospital, the
bodies were those of children and the scandal reached into
every single medical institution in the UK.

To appreciate their dilemma fully, archaeologists need to
understand why this medical crisis occurred. One of the obvious reasons is because the dead had become medical objects;
they were separated from their relatives and were transformed
from people into scientific specimens. But it is also important
to understand what the similarities are between the treatment
of the recently dead and the ancient dead. I would argue that
modern archaeology walks a fine line between arts, humanities
and science, but the burial part of modern archaeology has
undergone a massive scientific revolution since the middle of
the last century (Roberts 2009: 8-9): isotope analysis, forensic
pathology, studies in ancient DNA, to name just three developments. There has also been a substantial growth in university
courses in physical anthropology since the 1980s (Roberts
2009: 222), a popularity brought on by a series of key researchers and a general growth in interest in the forensic. This
has been an invaluable development within modern archaeology, as up to the early 1990s it was common to find skeletal
reports from cemetery project publications abridged, put into
microfiche, or listed as archive material. However, this transformation could also be described as a 'medicalisation' of death,
just as occurred at Alder Hey. It can be seen as objectifying

human body parts into scientific objects or data, whatever the feelings of the individual researchers, and by doing so it inherently delineates existing limitations on who has access to ancient remains.

The danger is that this objectification compartmentalises the dead into anthropological specimens, while others with an interest in the same dead do not understand or necessarily agree with archaeological criteria. An examination of the case studies in this book reveals not a change in attitude by archaeologists but a change in language, from Anne Mowbray who was of 'historic' interest, to the repatriation debates, to the reburial claims where human remains are of 'scientific' interest. However, the overuse of science can cause separation, just as surely as the walls and barriers erected around ongoing exhumation projects. It gives validity to the idea that our investigations are 'no more that experiments' and that archaeologists somehow tamper or fiddle with the dead in an inexplicable but deeply disturbing and unethical way.

The public may not necessarily understand the science of human remains, but they are interested in the dead and the stories the dead can tell. This disjunction between scientific and public archaeology needs to be broken; as shown in Chapters 1 and 2, there is no legal need for it to be an impermeable barrier: the ancient dead and their stories should be made more physically accessible. Projects like the Skeletons exhibition and Body Worlds have been hugely successful and influential in this area, and more ways to allow the public to participate beyond 'the armchair' can only strengthen archaeology and its purpose. But fundamentally a departmentalisation of scientific remains creates a separation and results in a dysfunctional relationship between the living and the dead. Where there is more than one interest in human remains this is very likely to lead to conflict in which the further the dead are separated from the living, the more external interest groups have a powerful point and public purpose.

To answer the question, who owns the stories about the dead: we should all own them. Open accessible projects have worked well in America; it is the projects that are disengaged that fail, or cause public humiliation. But this also means that it is important to publish the results of excavations. In two examples I have discussed, Rapparee Cove and Anne Mowbray, despite their respective public scandals, parliament was interested in archaeology because of the contribution that these cases could make to our collective understanding of the human experience, who we are and where we came from. However, in the cases of both Rapparee Cove and Anne Mowbray the questions raised again and again in parliament were about when these sites would be published: a question that is still unanswered.

Ethical frameworks

I have elected not to propose another ethical framework in this book: De Baets (2004), O'Sullivan (2001), Restall Orr & Bienkowski (2006b) are examples of those that have already been proposed, but there is a wider ethical context within which each case needs to be considered, including the individual guides of academic, museum and field practice institutions. The problem, it seems, is that there is not one single attitude from the public, or one single opinion about how human remains should be treated, that can be understood and adopted by all in a code of conduct. Ethical behaviour for one group of people may be deeply disturbing for another (see e.g. Smith & Wobst 2005). Equally an excavation that was, one week, perfectly acceptable, if done in another week may cause searching questions to be asked by a hostile media supported by a public protest movement. The situation is variable; each project and each exhibition has its own context, its own interest groups and its own circumstances, and so consultation is important. But more fundamentally, the ethical frameworks I have cited put the ancient bones first and what I have shown throughout this book is that, while the bones may matter to individuals, on the whole they are catalysts for other agendas tabled by the living. These agendas need to be understood before a suitable way forward can be found in any given situation, if that is possible at all once a conflict has arisen. One of the problems with ethical frameworks is that they are often inherently inflexible, proposed by individuals with a vested interest in a particular context, and so do not reflect the diversity of possible situations that may arise. On the other hand, they are important for industries and developers so that when issues arise there is a code of correct behaviour, lawful conduct and codes of practice.

Tarlow (2006) has already questioned the World Archaeology Congress's Vermillion Accord from within a British context: she argues that it is unsuitable and tends to favour New World countries, where there are often independent communities with distinguishable ancestors. The Vermillion Accord was adopted in 1989 at the WAC Inter-Congress, South Dakota, USA. It outlines six universal directives:

1. Respect for the mortal remains of the dead shall be accorded to all, irrespective of origin, race, religion, nationality, custom and tradition.
2. Respect for the wishes of the dead concerning disposition shall be accorded whenever possible, reasonable and lawful, when they are known or can be reasonably inferred.
3. Respect for the wishes of the local community and of relatives or guardians of the dead shall be accorded whenever possible, reasonable and lawful.
4. Respect for the scientific research value of skeletal, mummified and other human remains (including fossil hominids) shall be accorded when such value is demonstrated to exist.
5. Agreement on the disposition of fossil, skeletal, mummified and other remains shall be reached by negotiation on the basis of mutual respect for the legitimate concerns of communities for the proper disposition of their ancestors, as well as the legitimate concerns of science and education.
6. The express recognition that the concerns of various ethnic groups, as well as those of science are legitimate and to be respected, will permit acceptable agreements to be reached and honoured.

But there are further problems than simply the context which Tarlow raises. Often there are stark differences within commercial settings: archaeologists are forced to accept particular conditions to facilitate any involvement at all in cemetery clearance. For example, one of the questions posed throughout this book is whether a Methodist cemetery should be excavated to make way for a beer cellar. The easy answer, and the one which this accord would direct you to make is *no*. However, there are alternatives available: the law protecting human remains simply asks for their respectful treatment. So unless planning authorities place particular conditions on work, commercial clearance companies are still a viable alternative for the developer, and often cheaper than archaeology. Both industries have codes of conduct and definitions of what is and is not ethical. So what is more important in the Vermillion Accord, the custom and wishes of the dead (points 1 and 2), or the value of scientific research (point 4)? Additionally, there is no recourse in British law for the local authorities to consider point 3 through public consultation. In the case of more recent cemeteries a small advertisement may be placed in the local paper asking people who believe they are related to the cemetery occupants to come forward. Consequently the first a local community may know about the project is when the hoardings go up.

The Accord is important as it does not just get archaeologists to address important questions, but also considers indigenous communities. However, it implies that this is the only important relationship in modern archaeology, probably because, like the Native American Graves Protection and Repatriation Act, it was forged out of a particular situation, and like NAGPRA it does not have the flexibility to fit a diversity of situations.

There are other important relationships which need to be understood. I showed in Chapter 1 that the relationship between archaeology and the state, or lawmakers, is a very significant aspect of how human remains are, and will continue to be, treated. Another important relationship is that which exists between human remains and the general public (Chapter 4), and in Britain this extends beyond science and heritage but can also be an expression of the human experience and spirituality within a society where there are only a limited number of ways to experience the dead first hand. Other 'hard' sciences like astronomy have embraced their 'spiritual side' as part of their wider fascination and justification to the public. So maybe there does not have to be a natural juxtaposition between science and personal spirituality or religion among the museum-going or more general public, and actually there may not be, even among archaeologists, or students, particularly those who become interested in archaeology later in life. However, I would argue that trying to define what is sacred and profane (see Curtis 2004) simply misses the complexity of this relationship.

The Tamaki Makau-rau Accord is the most recent addition to the World Archaeology Congress codes of ethics and applies to the display of human remains. It was adopted in January 2006 and like the Vermillion Accord it also outlines six universal directives:

1. Permission should be obtained from the affected community or communities.
2. Should permission be refused that decision is final and should be respected.
3. Should permission be granted, any conditions to which that permission is subject should be complied with in full.
4. All display should be culturally appropriate.
5. Permission can be withdrawn or amended at any stage and such decisions should be respected.
6. Regular consultation with the affected community should ensure that the display remains culturally appropriate.

Similar problems as outlined for the Vermillion Accord are also present in this one. For example, when dealing with ancient and modern human remains, who are the affected communities? This is one of the reasons why Manchester Museum

(Chapter 4) is constantly asking the question, should human remains be displayed? Do they need to seek this constant permission from the general public, most of whom have specifically gone to see human remains? Indeed, the act of asking this question outside a structured environment can interfere with the appropriate display of those remains. In fact this Accord is even less relevant to a European setting than the Vermillion Accord because it is impossible to distinguish between affected communities and politically motivated interest groups. This provokes further questions: should a group's interest in an exhibition even be considered if it is driven by a political climate, rather than an actual cultural objection, especially as it will almost certainly be positioned in terms that raise a cultural objection?

The language used to discuss human remains between stakeholder communities is always emotive and always couched in terms of respect, even where there is no actual interest in the remains themselves. Clearly there are situations where Tamaki Makau-rau is relevant, for example the display of medieval Jews in a museum would be entirely inappropriate; the same would probably be regarded as true for other minority ethnic-religious groups, but what about Pagans, who are a religious group but not an ethnic one? Should ancient human remains be withdrawn from display because a single segment of society asks for this? Or is it important to have permission from a majority of people within north-western Europe who can claim ancestry to those remains? As a result, consultation processes should be wide and inclusive of many voices, an argument which is being made from within archaeology and museum studies and by Pagans. The case of Joan Wytte is a good example in which Pagan interests were important and relevant, but this body was withdrawn from display by an independent museum and reburial took place within the Pagan community. As independents they were under no obligation to follow the World Archaeology Congress agreements, but chose their own method to show Joan the respect they felt she deserved.

Conclusion

To further understand the problems that these Accords raise I would like to return to another case study, Rapparee Cove. I have outlined three interest groups: Britain's African diaspora, modern St Lucians, and archaeologists. The origin of the remains is still unresolved; however, let us assume they were Africans for a moment. One group wants the remains repatriated to their island home, and one would like them reburied with appropriate African rituals as a sign of respect to all slaves as part of the reparation movement. However, in this case there is a fourth interest group which is silent: the local community and the British people more generally. This is not a case where colonial collectors took the remains of the dead from a living community. The people died here. They are an important part of our British history – slavery was real. If they should be repatriated to St Lucia, should the Australian and North American governments likewise start the systematic identification and repatriation of first generation immigrants from the UK who were deported against their will? Clearly a ridiculous suggestion, but it fits within this context: how the wishes of the dead are regarded within global politics and global histories. It is sometimes less ethically correct to repatriate remains to minority groups, destroying past wrongs and pandering to 'post-colonial guilt', than it is to retain and remember.

There are problems with the application of the World Archaeology Congress codes of ethics outside the New World, just as there are with other codes and guides. This does not mean they are wrong; archaeologists both inside and outside Europe have found them very useful. Clearly having some general guides is important for a modern ethical profession which has many outside stakeholders with a shared interest in human remains and other artefacts. While I do not propose an ethical framework of my own, I do not desire to make others redundant, as that would be counterproductive. However, I would like to suggest some alternative principles which can be considered vital alongside organisational standards. One of the central arguments of this book is that each case is different. I

137

have also shown with Anne Mowbray, Fromelles, Bonn Square, Manhattan's African Burial Ground, Rapparee Cove and the other cases discussed that it is often secretiveness that causes problems for modern archaeology. As such it may be more appropriate for archaeologists, and archaeological organisations, to adopt the Seven Principles of Public Life when dealing with human remains. These are simply:

Selflessness
Integrity
Objectivity
Accountability
Openness
Honesty
Leadership

These principles require archaeologists to think beyond the profession, and beyond scholarship. They require independence from the scientific importance of a project while still requiring that individuals and projects are accountable to a scientific community. They ask for openness, accountability to all and objectivity in everything, and if appropriately applied at the beginning of a project they may help to reduce friction, heal hearts and safeguard scientific and public interests for the future. They require leadership from archaeologists who in that role may become facilitators to access rather than providing boundaries to contact. Most importantly they can be equally applied to research projects and commercial activities and may assist both to fulfil their wider social and academic importance. It would be worse, not just for archaeology but for society in general, if research projects, excavations, archaeological involvement in commercial projects, and the display of human remains came to an end. And I do not believe that this is the desire of any interest group or stakeholder community.

Bibliography

ACHP (1985). *Guidelines, for Consideration of Traditional Cultural Values in Historic Preservation Review,* Washington: Advisory Council on Historic Preservation.

Addeyman, P.V. (1994) 'Circumstances of excavation and research', in J.M. Lilly, G. Stroud, D.R. Brothwell & M.H. Williamson, *The Jewish Burial Ground at Jewbury, The Archaeology of York,* vol. 12: *The Medieval Cemeteries,* York: York Archaeology Trust.

Aldous, A. & Payne, S. (2009) 'London's buried bones: welcome reactions', *The Archaeologist* 72: 34-5.

Alport, C. (1965) 'Lord Alport, Removal of Anne Mowbray remains', *Hansard* 263: 120-3.

Andrews, L. & Nelkin, D. (1998) 'Whose body is it anyway? Disputes over body tissue in a biotechnology age', *Lancet* 351: 53-7.

Angel, J.L., Kelly, J.L., Parrington, M. & Pinter, S. (1987) 'Life stresses of the free black community as represented by the First African Baptist Church, Philadelphia, 1823-1841', *American Journal of Physical Anthropology* 74: 213-29.

Ariès, P. (1981) [1977] *The Hour of Our Death,* translated by H. Weaver, New York: Knopf.

ARM (2009) 'African Repatriation Movement' http://www.arm.arc.co.uk/home.html, accessed 19 November 2009.

Baker, S. (2008) 'Upper Chapel, Norfolk Street, Sheffield', Sheffield: unpublished ARCUS report 732f.3(1).

Banerjee, J. (2006) 'Thomas Hardy's poetry: the London years', *The Victorian Web* http://www.victorianweb.org/authors/hardy/banerjee.html, accessed 19 November 2009.

Barilan, Y.N. (2006) 'Body Worlds and the ethics of using human remains: a preliminary discussion', *Bioethics* 20(5): 233-47.

Barrow, P. (1998) *Slaves of Rapparee: The Wreck of the 'London',* Bideford: Lazarus Press.

Bashford, L. & Pollard, T. (1998) ' "In the burying place" – the excavation of a Quaker burial ground', in M. Cox (ed.) *Grave Concerns:*

Bibliography

Death and Burial in England 1700-1850, York: CBA Research Report 113.

BBC (1995) 'Bones of contention', a Films Media Group production for the BBC.

BBC (2001) 'Talking Point' http://news.bbc.co.uk/1/hi/talking_point/1144821.stm, accessed 19 November 2009.

BBC Look North (2009) 'Reburial service for Saxons', http://news.bbc.co.uk/player/nol/newsid_7280000/newsid_7283600/7283649.stm?bw=bb&mp=wm&news=1&nol_storyid=7283649&bbcws=1, accessed 19 November 2009.

Beaudry, M. (2009) 'Ethical issues in historic archaeology', in T. Majewski & D. Gaimster (eds) *International Handbook of Historical Archaeology*, London: Springer, 17-30.

Belford, P. & Witkin, A. (2000) 'Archaeological recording and osteological analysis of human remains from the site of the graveyard of St Paul's Church, Pinstone Street, Sheffield', Sheffield: unpublished ARCUS report, 323f.

Bell, L. & Lee-Thorp, J. (1998) 'Advances and constraints in the study of human remains: a joint perspective', in M. Cox (ed.) *Grave Concerns: Death and Burial in England 1700-1850*, York: CBA Research Report 113: 238-47.

Bergquist, A. (2001) 'Ethics and the archaeology of world religions', in T. Insoll (ed.) *Archaeology and World Religion*, London: Routledge, 182-90.

Bienkowski, P. (2009) 'Museum authority, knowledge and conflict', *Museum id,* http://www.museum-id.co.uk/museum_articledetails.asp?newsID=46, accessed 24 December 2009.

Blakey, M. (2001) 'Bioarchaeology of the African diaspora in the Americas: its origin and scope', *Annual Review of Anthropology* 30: 387-422.

Boore, E. (1998) 'Burial vaults and coffin furniture in the West Country', in M. Cox (ed.) *Grave Concerns: Death and Burial in England 1700-1850*, York: CBA Research Report 113: 67-84.

Boseley, S. (2000) 'Baby scandals "spell end of autopsies"', *Guardian*, 30 October.

Boston, C., Boyle, A., Gill, J. & Witkin, A. (2009) *'In the Vaults Beneath': Archaeological Recording at St George's Church Bloomsbury*, Oxford: Oxford Archaeology.

Boyle, A. (2004) 'What price compromise? Archaeological investigations at St Bartholomew's Church, Penn, Wolverhampton', *Church Archaeology* 5/6: 69-79.

Bibliography

Boyle, A. & Kevill, G. (1998) ' "To the praise of the dead, and anato-
mie": the analysis of post-medieval burials at St Nicholas,
Sevenoaks, Kent', in M. Cox (ed.) *Grave Concerns: Death and Burial in England 1700-1850;* York: CBA Research Report 113: 85-99.

Bradley, R.J. & Williams, H. (eds) (1998) 'The past in the past: the
reuse of ancient monuments', *World Archaeology* 30 (1), London:
Routledge.

Brickley, M., Buteux, S., Adams, J. & Cherrington, R. (2006) *St.
Martin's Uncovered: Investigations in the Churchyard of St. Martin's-in-the-Bull-Ring, Birmingham, 2001*, Oxford: Oxbow.

Brooks, M.M. & Rumsey, C. (2007) 'Who knows the fate of his bones?
Rethinking the body on display: object, art or human remains', in
S.J. Knell, S. MacLeod & S. Watson (eds) *Museum Revolutions:
How Museums Change and Are Changed*, Abingdon: Routledge:
343-54.

California Science Centre (2004) 'Body Worlds: An Anatomical Exhibition of Real Human Bodies'.

Carman, J. (2005) *Against Cultural Property*, London: Duckworth.

Carroll, Q. (2005) 'Bodies – who wants to rebury old skeletons?',
British Archaeology 82.

Carver, M.O.H. (con contributo di Gian Pietro Brogiolo) (2003) *Archaeological Value and Evaluation* (Manuali per l'Archeologia 2),
Mantova: Società Archeologica Padana.

Chadwick, E. (1843) *Report on the Sanitary Condition of the Labour-
ing Population of Great Britain. A Supplementary Report on the
Results of a Special Inquiry into the Practice of Interment in Towns*,
London: HMSO.

Chamberlin, A. & Parker Pearson, M. (2001) *Earthly Remains,* London: British Museum.

Chatters, J.C. (2002) *Ancient Encounters: Kennewick Man and the
First Americans*, New York: Simon & Schuster.

Chrisafis, A. (2002) 'Artist insists his bodies will survive legal fight',
Guardian, 12 March.

Chrisafis, A. (2009) 'French judge closes Body Worlds-style exhibition
of corpses', *Guardian,* 21 April.

Cohen, D. (1997) 'The bodies in question', *Independent*, 11 April.

Cohen, M. (1999a) 'Rapparee Cove, Devon', *Hansard* 333: 162.

Cohen, M. (1999b) 'Rapparee Cove, Devon', *Hansard* 336: 823.

Collins, V. (1965) 'Lord Stonham, removal of Anne Mowbray remains',
Hansard 263: 120-3.

Bibliography

Constable, N. & Farrington, K. (1997) 'Beach yields mass grave of shipwrecked slaves', *The Times*, 24 February.

Cox, M. (1998) 'Eschatology, burial practice and continuity: a retrospection from Christ Church, Spitalfields', in M. Cox (ed.) *Grave Concerns: Death and Burial in England 1700-1850*, York: CBA Research Report 113: 112-27.

Creative Sheffield (2007) *Top 10 Developments*, Sheffield: Sheffield City Council.

Curtis, N.G.W. (2004) 'Human remains: the sacred, museums and archaeology', *Public Archaeology* 3: 21-32.

Davidson, J.M. (2004) 'Mediating race and class through the death experience: power relations and resistance strategies of an African-American community, Dallas, Texas (1869-1907)', unpublished PhD thesis, University of Texas.

Davidson, J.M. (2007) 'Resurrection men in Dallas: the illegal use of black bodies as medical cadavers (1900-1907)', *International Journal of Historical Archaeology* 11(3): 193-220.

Dawes, M. (1993a) 'Screens fail to hide Supertram work in Cathedral grounds: staff shock at graveyard dig', *The Star* (Sheffield), 15 October.

Dawes, M. (1993b) 'No bones about it', *The Star* (Sheffield), 20 October.

DCA (2006) 'Burial law' http://www.dca.gov.uk/consult/buriallaw/buriallaw_cp0105.htm, accessed 29 April 2010.

De Baets, A. (2004) 'A declaration of the responsibilities of present generations toward past generations', *History and Theory, Theme Issue* 43: 130-64.

DiFranco, A. (1998) 'Fuel', 'Little Plastic Castle', Righteous Babe Records.

Dooks, B. (2009) 'Rituals of thousand years ago honour ancestors', *Yorkshire Post*, 5 October.

Draper, L. (1993) 'Excavation paves way for tram stop', *Sheffield Telegraph*, 8 September.

Emery, P. (2006) 'End of the line', *British Archaeology* 88.

Fairbank, W. (1771) 'A correct plan of the town of Sheffield in the County of York', Sheffield: Sheffield City Archive.

Fforde, C. (2002) 'Collection, repatriation and identity', in C. Fforde, J. Hubert & P. Turnbull (eds) *The Dead and Their Possessions: Repatriation in Principle, Policy and Practice*, London: Routledge: 25-46.

Bibliography

Fforde, C. (2004) *Collecting the Dead: Archaeology and the Reburial Issue*, London: Duckworth.

Fine-Dare, K.S. (2002) *Grave Injustice: The American Indian Repatriation Movement and NAGPRA*, Nebraska: University of Nebraska Press.

Fletcher, R. (1974) *The Akenham Burial Case*, London: Wildwood House.

French, A. (2008) 'Bonn Square skeletons to be reburied', *Oxford Times*, 30 January.

Garner, C. (1998) 'Witches finally lay old Joan to rest', *Independent*, 21 September.

Garrett-Frost, S. (1992) *The Law and Burial Archaeology*, Institute of Field Archaeologists Technical Paper 11.

Gerrard, C. (2003) *Medieval Archaeology*, Abingdon: Routledge.

Gibbs, G. (1997) 'Grant wants memorial to slaves', *Guardian*, 3 March 1997.

Giddens, A. (1991) *Modernity as Self-Identity: Self and Society in the Later Modern Age*, Cambridge: Cambridge University Press.

Gilchrist, R. (2003) 'Dust to dust: revealing the Reformation dead', in D. Gaimster & R. Gilchrist (eds) *The Archaeology of Reformation 1480-1580*, York: Maney, 399-414.

Goldman, J. (2006) 'Town unearths colonial slave cemetery', CBS Evening News, 13 February http://www.cbsnews.com/stories/ 2006/02/13/eveningnews/main1312816.shtml, accessed 19 November 2009.

Gosling, R. (1736) 'Sheffield from an Actual Survey', Sheffield: Sheffield City Archive.

Green, E. (1984) *Ethics and Values in Archaeology*, New York: The Free Press.

HAD (2007) 'Suffolk Survey Summer 2007' http://www.honour. org.uk/node/88, accessed 24 December 2007.

Harding, V. (1998) 'Research priorities: an historian's perspective', in M. Cox (ed.) *Grave Concerns: Death and Burial in England 1700-1850;* York: CBA Research Report 113: 203-5.

Harrington, S. (1993) 'Bones and bureaucrats', *Archaeology* 46(2): 28-38.

Harris, P. & Connolly, K. (2002) 'World trade in bodies is linked to corpse art show', *Guardian,* 17 March.

Henderson, M. (2006) 'Sending back of aboriginal bones "is loss to scientists"', *The Times,* 18 November.

143

Bibliography

Henderson, M. (2007) 'Museum surrenders vital clues to human evolution', *The Times*, 12 May.

Herald-Sun (2009) 'Australian soldiers in Fromelles, France, in limbo', *Herald-Sun*, 6 July.

Hey, D. (1998) *A History of Sheffield*, Lancaster: Carnegie Publishing.

Heys, T. (1945) *Sheffield Replanned*, Sheffield: Sheffield Town Planning Committee.

Historic Scotland (2006) *The Treatment of Human Remains in Archaeology: Historic Scotland Operational Policy Paper 5*, Edinburgh: Historic Scotland.

Houlbrooke, R. (1999) 'The Age of Decency: 1600-1760', in P.J. Jupp & C. Gittings (eds) *Death in England: An Illustrated History,* Manchester: Manchester University Press, 174-201.

Hubert, J. (1989) 'A proper place for the dead: a critical review of the "reburial" issue', in R. Layton (ed.) *Conflict in the Archaeology of Living Traditions*, London: Unwin Hyman, 131-66.

Hunter, J. (1869) [revised by A. Gatty from the 1819 edition] *Hallamshire: The History and Topography of the Parish of Sheffield in the County of York*, Sheffield: Pawson and Brailsford.

Hunter, J. & Ralston, I. (1993) 'The structure of British archaeology', in J. Hunter & I. Ralston, *Archaeological Resource Management in the UK: An Introduction,* Stroud: Sutton.

Hurst, T.D. (2000) *Skull Wars: Kennewick Man, Archaeology, and the Battle for Native American Identity*, New York: Basic Books.

Hutton, K. (2009) Reburying Albert Camus: a political ploy by Sarkozy? *Time*, 24 November.

Hutton, R. (2001) *The Triumph of the Moon: A History of Modern Pagan Witchcraft*, Oxford: Oxford University Press.

Hutton, R. (2007) *The Druids*, London: Hambledon Continuum.

Hutton, R. (2009) *Blood and Mistletoe: The History of the Druids in Britain*, New Haven: Yale University Press.

IFA (1981) *Institute of Field Archaeology: Code of Conduct.*

Institute for Plastination (2009) 'The Unparalleled Success, Gunther von Hagens' Body Worlds, The Original Exhibition of Real Human Bodies' http://www.bodyworlds.com/en/exhibitions/unparallelled_success.html, accessed 19 November.

Jackson, K (2002) 'Body Worlds: Dr Frankenstein, I presume', *Independent*, 9 March.

Jeffries, S. (2002) 'The naked and the dead', *Guardian*, 19 March.

Jenkins, T. (2008) 'Dead bodies: the changing treatment of human remains in British museum collections and the challenge to the traditional model of the museum', *Mortality* 13(2): 105-18.

Jones, P.N. (2005). *Respect for the Ancestors: American Indian Cultural Affiliation in the American West*, Boulder: Bauu Institute.

Karacs, I. (1998) 'Arts: body art tests limits of taste', *Independent*, 15 January.

Kennedy, H. (2006) 'Knowledge or humanity', *Guardian*, 28 March.

Kennedy, M. (2008) 'The great mummy cover-up', *Guardian*, 23 May.

Kilmister, H. (2003) 'Visitor perceptions of Ancient Egyptian human remains in three United Kingdom museums', *Papers from the Institute of Archaeology* 14: 57-69.

Kirby, D. (2007) 'Lindow Man comes home to his roots', *Manchester Evening News*, 29 January.

Kirk, L. & Start, H. (1999) 'Death at the undertakers', in J. Downs & T. Pollard (eds) *The Loved Bodies Corruption: Archaeological Contributions to the Study of Human Mortality*, Glasgow: Cruithne Press.

Klesert, A. & Andrews, M. (1988) 'The treatment of human remains on Navajo lands', *American Antiquity* 53(2): 310-20.

Klesert, A. & Powell, S. (1993) 'A perspective on ethics and the reburials controversy', *American Antiquity* 58(2): 348-54.

L'Indépendent (2007) 'La dépouille de Mgr Dillon suscite un élan de ferveur', *L'Indépendent,* 17 April.

La Roche, C.J. & Blakey, M.L. (1997) 'Seizing intellectual power: the dialogue at the New York African Burial Ground', *Historical Archaeology* 31(3): 84-106.

Leader, R.E. (1875) *Reminiscences of Old Sheffield: Its Streets and Its People*, Sheffield: Leader.

Leake, J. (2000) 'Graves to be dug up and reused after 50 years', *Sunday Times,* 23 April.

Levin, B. (1984) 'If these bones lie at peace civilisation may surely rest', *The Times*, 11 January.

Live News (2009) 'Rudd denies archaeologists cut corners in Fromelles exhumation', livenews.com.au, 6 July.

Logie, J. (1992) 'Appendix Four: Scots Law', in S. Garrett-Frost, *The Law and Burial Archaeology*, Institute of Field Archaeologists Technical Paper 11: 11-15.

Mackenzie, B. (1966) 'Lord Amulree, remains of Anne Mowbray, Duchess of York', *Hansard* 276: 1680-1.

Mahoney-Swales, D., O'Neill, R. & Willmott, H. (forthcoming) 'The hidden material culture of death: coffins and grave goods in late

Bibliography

18th and early 19th century Sheffield', in C. King & D Sayer (eds) *The Archaeology of Post-Medieval Religion*, Woodbridge: Boydell.

Manchester Museum (2007) *The Manchester Museum: Strategic Plan for 2007-2010*, Manchester: University of Manchester.

Manchester Museum (2009) 'Criticism, Lindow Manchester' http://lindowmanchester.wordpress.com/category/criticism/, accessed 19 November 2009.

Manning, J.E. (1900) *History of Upper Chapel, Sheffield*, Sheffield: The Independent Press.

Marshall, D. (2009) 'Corpseshow' http://petitions.number10.gov.uk/corpseshow/, accessed 19 November 2009.

Mays, S. (2005) (ed.) *Guidance for Best Practice for the Treatment of Human Remains Excavated from Christian Burial Grounds in England*, London: English Heritage & Church of England.

McIntyre, L. & Willmott, H. (2003) 'Excavations at the Methodist Chapel Carver Street Sheffield', Sheffield: unpublished ARCUS report 507.

McKie, R. (2008), 'Anger as burial site digs are blocked', *Observer*, 2 March.

McManamon, F.P. (2004) 'Kennewick Man' http://www.nps.gov/archeology/kennewick/, accessed 19 November 2009.

McMullin, R. (2006) 'Disaster at Fromelles', *Wartime Magazine* 36.

Miles, A., Powers, N., Wroe-Brown, R. & Walker, D. (2008) *St Marylebone Church and Burial Ground in the 18th to 19th Centuries: Excavations as St Marylebone School 1992, and 2004-6*, MoLAS Monograph 46, London: Museum of London Archaeology Service.

Miles, A., White, W. & Tankard, D. (2008) *Burial at the Site of the Parish Church of St Benet Sherehog Before and After the Great Fire: Excavations at 1 Poultry, City of London*, MoLAS Monograph 39, London: Museum of London Archaeology Service.

Mills, S & Tranter, V. (2010) *Research into Issues Surrounding Human Bones in Museums*, London: English Heritage.

MoJ (2008) 'Ministry of Justice and Burials' http://www.archaeologists.net/modules/news/article.php?storyid=489, accessed 29 April 2010.

Molleson, T. (1987) 'Anne Mowbray and the Princes in the Tower: a study in historical identity', *London Archaeologist* 5 (10): 258-62.

Molleson, T. (2002) 'Anne Mowbray and the skeletons in the Tower', in P. Bahn (ed.) *Written in Bones: How Human Remains Unlock the Secrets of the Dead*, London: Quintet, 151-4.

Molleson, T. & Cox, M. (1993) *The Spitalfields Project,* vol. 2: *The Anthropology; The Middling Sort,* CBA Research Report 86.

Moorhen, W. (2005) 'Anne Mowbray: in life and death', *Ricardian Bulletin,* Spring.

Morris, R. (1994) 'Examine the dead gently', *British Archaeology,* October, 9.

Morris, S. & Constable, N. (2007) 'Prisoners or slaves? New row over wreck's bones', *Guardian,* 6 November.

Moshenska, G. (2009) 'The reburial issue in Britain', *Antiquity* 83: 815-20.

Moss, S. (2009) 'My day with the relics of Saint Thérèse of Lisieux', *Guardian,* 14 October.

Museum of Witchcraft (2009) 'Full Record: Museum No. 24' http://www.museumofwitchcraft.com/displayrecord_mow.php?Ob jectNumber=24, accessed 19 November 2009.

Museums Association (2008) *Code of Ethics for Museums: Ethical Principles for All Who Work for or Govern Museums in the UK,* London: Museums Association.

NAGPRA (1990) Native American Graves Protection and Repatriation Act, *Federal Register 2005* 70(169): 5066-8.

Neuburg, V. (1985) *London Labour and the London Poor,* London: Penguin Classics.

O'Neill, R., Baker, K. & Swales, D. (2007) 'Assessment report of archaeological excavations at Sheffield Cathedral NW car park, Sheffield, South Yorkshire', Sheffield: unpublished ARCUS report 546d.1.

O'Sullivan, J. (2001) 'Ethics and the archaeology of human remains', *Journal of Irish Archaeology* X: 121-51.

Observer (1965) 'The world of Lady Anne Mowbray', *Observer,* 23 May.

Office for National Statistics (2004) 'KS01 Usual resident population: Census 2001, Key statistics for urban areas', London: Office for National Statistics.

Owsley, D.W. & Jantz, R.L. (2002) 'Kennewick Man – a kin? Too distant', in E. Barkan & R. Bush (eds), *Claiming the Stones, Naming the Bones: Cultural Property and the Negotiation of National and Ethnic Identity,* Los Angeles: Getty Publications: 141-61.

Oxford Archaeology (2008) 'Bonn Square, Oxford' http://thehumanjourney.net/index.php?option=com_content&task= view&id=371&Itemid=40, accessed 19 November 2009.

Oxford Archaeology (2009) 'Remembering Fromelles' http://thehumanjourney.net/index.php?option=com_content&task =view&id=501&Itemid=40, accessed 19 November 2009.

Bibliography

Oxford Mail (2008a) 'Bones find as site is cleared', *Oxford Mail*, 30 January.

Oxford Mail (2008b) 'Bonn Square skeletons to be reburied: Forum' http://www.oxfordmail.net/search/display.var.2006673.0.bonn_square _skeletons_to_be_reburied.php, accessed 19 November 2009.

Parker Pearson, M. (1993) 'The powerful dead: archaeological relationships between the living and the dead', *Cambridge Archaeological Journal* 3(2): 203-29.

Parker Pearson, M. (1999) *The Archaeology of Death and Burial*, Stroud: Sutton.

Parrington, M. & Roberts, D.G. (1984) 'The First African Baptist Cemetery', *Archaeology* 37(6): 26-32.

Payne, S. (2009) 'Is it right to excavate and study human remains?: re-examining the issues of Jewbury', *The Archaeologist* 72: 42-3.

Pitchforth, J. (ed.) (2004a) *The Small Guide to the Parishes in the Sheffield Area*, Sheffield: Sheffield and District Family History Society.

Pitchforth, J. (ed.) (2004b) *The Small Guide to Nonconformist and Roman Catholic Churches in Sheffield*, Sheffield: Sheffield and District Family History Society.

Pitts, M. (2006) 'Bling king's last battle', *British Archaeology* 88.

Purves, L. (2008) 'Please – enough of this ghoulish sideshow', *The Times*, 6 October.

Rahtz, P. (1991) *Invitation to Archaeology*, Oxford: Blackwell.

Randerson, J. (2007) 'Give us back our bones, pagans tell museums', *Guardian*, 5 February.

Redfern, M., Keeling, J. & Powell, E. (2001) *The Royal Liverpool Children's Inquiry, Report* (full text available at http://www.rlcinquiry.org.uk/download/appen.pdf)

Rees Leahy, H. (2008) 'Under the skin', *Museum Practice* 43: 36-40.

Reeve, J. (1998) 'A view from the metropolis: post-medieval burials in London', in M. Cox (ed.) *Grave Concerns: Death and Burial in England 1700-1850*, York: CBA Research Report 113: 213-38.

Reeve, J. & Adams, M. (1993) *The Spitalfields Project*, vol. 1: *Across the Styx*, York: CBA Research Report 85.

Rescue News (2003) 'St Pancras Cemetery a lesson to learn', *Rescue News*.

Restall Orr, E. (2008) 'Lindow Man in Manchester: on display' http://www.honour.org.uk/node/87, accessed 19 November 2009.

Restall Orr, E. & Bienkowski, P. (2006a). 'Respect for all', *Museums Journal* 106/7: 18.

Bibliography

Restall Orr, E. & Bienkowski, P. (2006b) 'Respectful treatment and reburial: a practical guide', unpublished paper delivered to the Respect for Ancient British Human Remains: Philosophy and Practice conference at Manchester Museum on 7 November 2006 http://www.museum.manchester.ac.uk/medialibrary/documents/respect/respect_practical_guide.pdf , accessed 19 November 2009.

Riccardi, N. (2009) 'Utah town's anger mounts over artifact arrests', *Los Angeles Times*, 17 June.

Riccardi, N. & Tankersley, J. (2009) '24 charged in crackdown on Native American artifact looting', *Los Angeles Times,* 11 June.

Roberts, C. (2009) *Human Remains in Archaeology: A Handbook*, CBA Practical Handbook 19, York: Council for British Archaeology.

Roberts, C.A. & Cox, M. (2003) *Health and Disease in Britain: Prehistory to the Present Day*, Gloucester: Sutton Publishing.

Roberts, D.G. & McCarthy, J.P. (1995) 'Descendant community partnering in the archaeological and bioanthropological investigation of African-American skeletal populations: two interrelated case studies from Philadelphia', in A.L. Grauer (ed.) *Bodies of Evidence: Reconstructing History Through Skeletal Analysis*, New York: Wiley, 19-36.

Rogers, E. (2009) 'Fromelles remains safe in our hands: Rudd', ABC News, 6 July. http://www.abc.net.au/news/stories/2009/07/06/2617627.htm, accessed 19 November 2009.

RPS (2009) News http://www.rpsgroup.com/Group/News/February-2008/Kings-Cross-Central-and-Brent-Cross-are-Winners.aspx, accessed 29 April 2010.

Rushton, M. A. (1965) 'The teeth of Anne Mowbray', *British Dental Journal* 119(8): 355-9.

Sarre, J. (2002) 'Boudicca and King's Cross Station' http:// www.museumoflondon.org.uk/English/Learning/Learningonline/features/roman/roman_london_7.htm, accessed 19 November 2009.

Sawday, J. (1997) 'Livid and the dead', *Times Higher Education Supplement,* 18 April.

Sayer, D. (2001) 'Sheffield Cathedral Cemetery', Sheffield: Report for ARCUS.

Sayer, D. (2009) 'Is there a crisis facing British burial archaeology?' *Antiquity* 83: 199-205.

Sayer, D. (2010) 'Who's afraid of the dead? Archaeology, modernity and the death taboo', *World Archaeology* 42 (3).

Sayer, D. (forthcoming) 'Death and the Dissenter: group identity and stylistic simplicity as witnessed in 19th-century Nonconformist gravestones', *Historic Archaeology*.

Sayer, D. & Symonds, J. (2004) 'Lost congregations: the crisis facing later post-medieval urban burial grounds', *Church Archaeology* 5/6: 55-61.

Sayer, D. & Williams, H. (2009) (eds) *Mortuary Practices and Social Identities in the Middle Ages*, Exeter: University of Exeter Press.

Scarre, C. (2006) 'Can archaeology harm the dead?', in C. Scarre & G. Scarre (eds) *The Ethics of Archaeology*, Cambridge: Cambridge University Press: 181-98.

Scarre, C. & Scarre, G. (2006) (eds) *The Ethics of Archaeology*, Cambridge: Cambridge University Press.

Scarre, G. (2007) *Death: Central Problems of Philosophy*, Stocksfield: Acumen.

Schofield, J. (2008) 'Lindow Man: Manchester Museum gets bogged down', http://www.manchesterconfidential.com/index.asp?Sessionx =IpqiNwImNwIjIDY6IHqjNwB6IA, accessed 19 November 2009.

Searle, A. (2002) 'Getting under the skin', *Guardian*, 23 March.

Sengupta, K. (1998) 'Jail for sculptor who stole body parts', *Independent*, 4 April 1998.

Sheffield Hallam University (2009) 'Hadfield, Mathew: "Cholera Monument"' http://public-art.shu.ac.uk/sheffield/unk126.html, accessed 19 November 2009.

Shepherd, N. (2007) 'Archaeology dreaming: post-apartheid urban imaginations and the bones of the Prestwich Street dead', *Journal of Social Archaeology* 7: 3-28.

Skeates, R. (2000) *Debating the Archaeological Heritage*, London: Duckworth; Debates in Archaeology series.

Small, J. (2008) 'Archaeologists' fear over burial law', *The Press*, 4 March.

Smith, C. & Wobst, H.M. (2005) (eds) *Indigenous Archaeologies: Decolonizing Theory and Practice*, New York: Routledge.

Smith, G. (2002) 'Graves destroyed by Chunnel diggers', *Evening Standard*, 26 December.

Smith, L-J. (2004) 'The repatriation of human remains – problems or opportunity', *Antiquity* 78: 404-12.

Smith, M. & Mays, S. (2007). 'Ancestors of us all', *Museums Journal*, January: 18.

Smith, S.D. (2006) *Slavery, Family, and Gentry Capitalism in the British Atlantic*, Cambridge: Cambridge University Press.

Stock, G. (1998) 'The 18th and early 19th century Quaker burial ground at Bathford, Bath and North East Somerset', in M. Cox (ed.) *Grave Concerns: Death and Burial in England 1700-1850*, York: CBA Research Report 113: 144-53.

SYHEC (2009) 'South Yorkshire Historic Environment Characterisation' http://www.sytimescapes.org.uk/home, accessed 19 November 2009.

Tarlow, S. (2006) 'Archaeology ethics and the people of the past', in C. Scarre & G. Scarre (eds) *The Ethics of Archaeology*, Cambridge: Cambridge University Press: 199-216.

Thackray, D. & Payne, S. (2008) 'Draft report on the request for the reburial of human remains from the Alexander Keiller Museum at Avebury' http://www.english-heritage.org.uk/upload/pdf/Draft_report .pdf?1258613459, accessed 19 November 2009.

Thornton, R. (2002) 'Repatriation as healing the wounds of the trauma of history: cases of Native Americans in the United States of America', in C. Fforde, J. Hubert & P. Turnbull (eds) *The Dead and Their Possessions: Repatriation in Principle, Policy and Practice*, London: Routledge, 17-24.

Totaro, P. (2009) 'Cheap choice derails graves project', *Brisbane Times/Sydney Morning Herald*, 6 July.

Tucker, A. (2009) 'Burial law reform and archaeology', *The Archaeologist* 72: 30.

Vanden-Bempde-Johnstone, P. (1965) 'Lord Derwent, reinterment of Anne Mowbray remains', *Hansard* 264: 182-5.

Verdery, K. (1999) *The Political Lives of Dead Bodies: Reburial and Postsocialist Change*, New York: Columbia University Press.

Vickers, J.E. (1978) *A Popular History of Sheffield*, Wakefield: EP Publishing.

Vine, S. (2008) 'Skeletons: London's Buried Bones at the Wellcome Collection', *The Times,* 23 July.

Wallis, R. & Blain, J. (2004) 'No one voice', *British Archaeology* 78: 10-13.

Walter, T. (1994) *The Revival of Death*, London: Routledge.

Walter, T. (2004a) 'Plastination for display: a new way to dispose of the dead', *Journal of the Royal Anthropological Institute* 19(3): 603-27.

Walter, T. (2004b) 'Body Worlds: clinical detachment and anatomical awe', *Sociology of Health & Illness* 26(4): 464-88.

Walter, T. (2005) 'Three ways to arrange a funeral: mortuary variation in the modern West', *Mortality* 10(3): 173-92.

Bibliography

Walter, T. (2008) 'To see for myself: informed consent and the culture of openness', *Journal of Medical Ethics* 34(9): 675-8.

Walter, T. (forthcoming) 'Seventeen ways to view a corpse', in G. Howarth (ed.) *Modern Death*, London: Reaktion Books.

Watson, B. & White, W. (forthcoming) *Anne Mowbray, Duchess of York: A 15th Century Child Burial for the Minories, London.*

Webb, S. (1987) 'Reburying Australian skeletons', *Antiquity* 61: 292-6.

Weeks, J. & Bott, V. (2003) 'Scoping survey of historic human remains in English museums', London: Department for Culture, Media and Sport, Cultural Property Unit.

Wheeler, P. (1999) 'A survey of cemeteries in Sheffield', unpublished dissertation, University of Sheffield, Department of Lifelong Learning.

White, B. (1998) 'The excavation and study of human remains: a view from the floor', in M. Cox (ed.) *Grave Concerns: Death and Burial in England 1700-1850*, York: CBA Research Report 113: 247-52.

White, B. (2009) 'An advisory panel for the archaeology of all burials in England', *The Archaeologist* 72: 28-9.

Whitney, A. (2001) 'St Lucia stakes its claim to the bones of the "heroic rebels" of Rapparee Cove', *Independent*, 8 February.

Wilkinson, J. & Coleman, B. (2001) 'The legal and ethical consideration relating to the supply and use of human tissue for biomedical research: a UK perspective', *Journal of Commercial Biotechnology*: 8(2): 140-6.

Yardley, W. (2009) 'Indian artefact looting case unsettles a Utah town', *New York Times,* 21 June.

Zarchin, T. & Eyadat, F. (2009) 'Israelis protest Haifa showing of "Body Worlds" exhibit', *Haaretz*, 28 June.

Zimmerman, L.J. (1987) 'Webb on reburial: a North American perspective', *Antiquity* 61: 462-3.

Zimmerman, L.J. (1989) 'Made radical by my own', in R. Layton (ed.) *Conflict in the Archaeology of Living Traditions*, London: Unwin Hyman, 60-7.

Index

Act of Parliament, 26, 37, 40

African Burial Ground, New York, 70, 72-5, 82, 91, 93-4, 129, 138

African Repatriation Movement (ARM), 76-7

Alder Hey, 14, 59, 63, 98, 108, 128, 130

Alexander Keiller Museum, Avebury, 120, 122, 123

America, 10, 66, 70-5, 87, 95-8, 109-13, 116, 120, 124, 127, 132, 134, 137

Anatomy Act, 46

anatomy museums, 60, 63, 100, 109

Atlantis Gallery, 98

Australia, 10, 61, 89, 90, 91, 95, 109, 110, 113-16, 120, 124, 127, 129, 137

Australian High Commission, 114

Australian High Court, 61

Beth Din, 80-1

Birmingham city archaeologists, 55

Manchester, Bishop of, 100

Body Worlds, 17, 96, 97-100, 106, 109, 125, 129, 131

Bonn Square, Oxford, 71, 87-9, 91-4, 129-30, 138

Bradford University, 114

Bristol Hospital, 59

British Association for Biological Anthropology and Osteoarchaeology (BABAO), 62-3

British Museum, 107, 114

Broad Lane Quaker Cemetery, Sheffield, 27-9, 35

Burial Act, 35, 45, 46, 48, 51, 56, 80, 81

burial law, 15, 36, 42, 45-64, 66, 67, 69, 127, 128

Cambridge Archaeology, 107

Camus, Albert, 15

Carver Street Methodist Chapel, Sheffield, 9, 28, 29, 35, 36, 38, 40, 41, 43, 82, 83

Channel Tunnel Rail Link (CTRL), 39, 86

Cholera Burial Ground, Sheffield, 28, 29, 34

Church of England, 15, 55, 86

common law, 36, 46, 47, 57, 61, 64, 66, 67, 69

Council for British Archaeology (CBA), 47, 49, 55, 86

Index

Council of British Druid Orders (CoBDO), 120, 123

Department of Constitutional Affairs, 55
Department of Culture, Media and Sport, 63
DiFranco, Ani, 70, 73
Dillon, Arthur, 11, 117-18
disarticulated bones, 68
Disused Burial Grounds Amendment, 35, 46, 48, 51

eBay, 63, 65
English Heritage, 47, 54-6, 86, 123
exhumation companies, 36, 39, 47, 71, 84-6

Faculty of the Ordinary, 46, 51, 66
First African Baptist Churchyard, Philadelphia, 72
foetus, 59, 61, 62
France, 15, 71, 89, 90, 96, 117
Freedman's cemetery, Dallas, 74,
Fromelles, Northern France, 71, 89, 90, 93-4, 129, 130, 138

General Cemetery, Sheffield, 28, 29-30, 34
Germany, 58, 90, 96, 106, 116, 122
Gifford, 39, 86, 87
Glasgow Art Gallery, 114
grave-goods, 64-5, 119, 126
Guidance for Best Practice for the Treatment of Human Remains Excavated from Christian Burial Grounds in England, 55, 123

Hardy, Thomas, 45
Her Majesty's Inspector of Anatomy, 60
Historic Scotland, 58, 64, 97, 123
Home Office, 36, 39, 45-7, 49, 50, 52, 56, 80, 81
Honouring the Ancient Dead (HAD), 95, 107, 120
House of Commons, 37, 54
House of Lords, 53
Howard Street Congregational Church, Sheffield, 28, 30, 34
Human Tissue Act, 46, 60, 62, 63, 67, 68, 113, 114, 116, 122, 127
Human Tissue Authority (HTA), 60, 62-3, 97

Infirmary Cemetery, Sheffield, 28, 30, 35, 38
Institute for Archaeologists (IfA), 47, 49
Israel, 96

Jewbury, York, 71, 79-83, 92, 118, 119, 127, 129

Kelly, Anthony-Noel, 60, 61, 63, 98, 128
Kennewick Man, 58, 111, 112, 129

licence to remove human remains, 35, 36, 39, 46-58, 66, 68, 81-4
Lindow Man, 102-6, 125, 129
Living Cemetery Project, 54

Manchester Museum, 102-6, 109, 125, 129, 135
medicalisation of death, 108, 130

Ministry of Justice, 46-8, 54, 56, 58, 66
Mowbray, Anne, 46, 49-53, 57, 58, 67, 118, 128, 131, 132, 138
Museum of London, 49, 59, 86, 100
Museum of the Phrenological Society, Edinburgh, 113
Museum of Witchcraft, 119
museum: feedback, 101-4
museum: role of, 18, 105, 106, 108, 109, 115, 116, 123, 129
Museums Association Code of Ethics, 123

Narbonne Cathedral, 117
National Museum of the American Indian Act, 111
National Slavery Memorial Day, 76
National Trust, 123
Native American Graves Protection and Repatriation Act (NAGPRA), 71, 111, 134
Native Americans, 71, 110-13
Nether Chapel, Sheffield, 28, 30-1, 34
Newman, John Henry, 15-16

objects (bones as), 13, 69, 130-1
ownership of human remains, 58-64, 67, 69, 124, 128, 130
Oxford Archaeology, 39, 87-91

Pagan Federation, 121
Pagans for Archaeology, 120-1
Parliament, 50, 52, 67, 76, 132
Peterborough City Museum, 114
Pitt Rivers Museum, Oxford, 114
Plain Roundabout, Oxford, 88
plastination, 97-100, 108

police, 36, 49, 51, 60, 61
portable antiquities scheme, 65
pre-Christian burial, 56, 107
Pre-Construct Archaeology (PCA), 39, 86
Prestwich Street, Cape Town, South Africa, 78
Prittlewell, Southend, 88-9
Public Bodies Liaison Committee for British Paganism (PEBBLE), 122
Public Law, 102-3, 73
public opinion, 71, 93

Queen Street Chapel, Sheffield, 28, 30, 35

rabbi, 79, 80, 92
Rapparee Cove, Devon, 71, 75-8, 91, 94, 129, 132, 137, 138
reburial, 46, 47, 49-53, 56-7, 71-3, 75-6, 81, 83, 88, 108-12, 117-25, 129, 131, 136
reinterpretation (of the British burial laws), 16, 46-9, 54, 56, 64, 66, 128
repatriation (New World), 71, 76-7, 95, 109-16, 124
repatriation (Old World), 95, 113-18, 125
RESCUE, 40, 53, 86
respect, 16, 17, 58, 60, 63, 68, 70, 72, 74, 79-82, 87, 91, 96, 98, 102, 104, 107, 110, 118, 119, 122-6, 129, 133-7
right of sepulchre, 58
Rossetti, Dante Gabriel, 66
Royal Collage of Pathologists, 59-60
Royal College of Surgeons, 60-1, 114

sale of human remains, 58, 62-3
Science Museum, 113-15
Scottish law, 54, 58, 60, 68
screening of remains, 36, 43-4,
   84, 88
Seven Principles of Public Life,
   138
Shambles Museum, 62
Sheffield Cathedral, 28, 29,
   32-3, 35, 37, 40, 44, 83-5, 87,
   93
Skeletons, London's Buried
   Bones, 44, 100-2, 106, 125,
   129, 131
South Africa, 10, 78, 93-4, 127
St Albans Abbey, St Albans, 83,
   118
St Clement's, Oxford, 88
St George's, Sheffield, 28, 31, 34
St John's Park, Sheffield, 28, 31,
   35
St Lucia, Caribbean, 75-7, 137
St Martin's Church,
   Birmingham, 39
St Mary's Church, Masham,
   North Yorkshire, 119
St Mary's Church, Sheffield, 28,
   31, 35
St Paul's Church, Sheffield, 28,
   31, 35, 38

St Peter's Church,
   Barton-upon-Humber, North
   Lincolnshire, 119
St Philip's Cemetery, Sheffield,
   28, 32, 35

Tamaki Makau-rau Accord, 96,
   111, 135, 136
Tasmania, 113-16
Terracotta Army exhibition, 100
theft (of human remains), 61,
   63, 109, 115
Treasure Act, 59, 64-5
Treasures of Tutankhamen, 100

University of Edinburgh, 114
Upper Chapel, Sheffield, 28, 30,
   34

Vermillion Accord, 110-11, 133-6

Wellcome Trust, 100, 106
Westminster Abbey, 50, 118
World Archaeology Congress,
   96, 110, 111, 133, 135-7
Wytte, Joan, 119, 136

York Archaeological Trust,
   79-80, 82